PENINSULAR PORTRAIT

your dutiful Son
William Bragge

I. Captain William Bragge at the age of thirty-six.
From a miniature painted in 1824.

PENINSULAR PORTRAIT

1811-1814

The Letters of
Captain William Bragge
Third (King's Own) Dragoons

EDITED BY

S. A. C. CASSELS
Commander, Royal Navy.

London
OXFORD UNIVERSITY PRESS
NEW YORK, TORONTO
1963

Oxford University Press, Amen House, London E.C. 4

GLASGOW NEW YORK TORONTO MELBOURNE WELLINGTON
BOMBAY CALCUTTA MADRAS KARACHI LAHORE DACCA
CAPE TOWN SALISBURY NAIROBI IBADAN ACCRA
KUALA LUMPUR HONG KONG

Printed in Great Britain

To my Godson

CHRISTOPHER

May he enjoy his
great-great-grandfather's
letters and share his
taste for adventure

Contents

Illustrations

Maps

Preface

The existence of an abridged manuscript copy of Captain William Bragge's Letters from the Peninsula was known to a few of his descendants for many years. Little attention had been paid to it, though; in fact its whereabouts had long been uncertain and its contents forgotten. The unexpected discovery of the original Letters in the home of the late Captain O. C. Bragge of Hawkchurch, Devon, in the summer of 1958 aroused renewed interest in them, especially when the character of William Bragge's writing was revealed.

The writer of these Letters (the originals of which are now in the possession of Mrs. G. K. Bantoft of Umtali, Southern Rhodesia) was the eldest son of a Dorset squire and came from a line long established in the County. He went to the Peninsula as a very junior Lieutenant of twenty-three serving in the 3rd (King's Own) Dragoons. When he left England he had never known a world really at peace; even so, after the quiet, orderly life of his home, war-torn Portugal and savage, mutilated Spain were a rude awakening to army service overseas. He found his feet quickly, however, making the most of his circumstances as an alert and promising officer. From Lisbon in the exhausting summer heat of 1811, he shared the fortunes of Wellington's Army through the brilliant Salamanca campaign and the galling withdrawal from Burgos in 1812, and the signal defeat of the French at Vitoria in 1813. In the same year he obtained his Troop of Horse and was officially gazetted Captain. He was recalled to England the following year just as the Allied armies were closing in on Toulouse and landed at Plymouth to the joyful news of Napoleon's abdication.

During this period of just over two and a half years William Bragge wrote about forty letters to his father, of which thirty-eight reached him at Sadborow, the family home in Dorset, and have survived. He also wrote several letters to other members of his family, of which only one to his brother-in-law has been preserved. These are the thirty-nine letters in this book.

The Letters are of interest not only as one of the few personal records from a cavalry regiment covering nearly the whole of its period on active service in the Peninsula—the majority of the published narratives have been from the infantry—but also because they reflect so vividly a junior officer's impressions of his surroundings and his attitude to army life in ever-changing campaign conditions, with all his private hopes and disappointments expressed in confidence and sincerity to an indulgent father. He was a shrewd, mature and surprisingly accurate observer, sparing his reader only the more revolting details of the filth, squalor and sickness which he had to endure. He may not reveal any startling new facts about a well-documented period but some minor points are noteworthy, and from his junior position he puts forward an ingenious interpretation of Wellington's preliminary moves before the opening of the campaign of 1813. And when from time to time he allows himself the luxury of a derisory remark about his superiors, it is not without a large measure of justification. With a few notable exceptions, Wellington was poorly served by many of his Commanders—in fact William Bragge further corroborates the impressions which have been gained from other sources. Wellington is among the few to escape his barbs, for it is evident that he had implicit faith in and respect for his Commander-in-Chief.

The Letters also emphasize indirectly the complete absence of any form of censorship, with the result that occasionally a Dorset squire may have been temporarily better informed than the Secretary of State for War waiting for Wellington's fuller but later dispatch, for Wellington was notoriously reticent about his intentions and rarely explained them until they could not possibly be countermanded from London. If the Packet returning to England was by mischance intercepted by a French or American Man-of-war, the mails were merely thrown overboard and sometimes even this precaution was overlooked. It is evident too, how much the regularity of the Lisbon-Falmouth Packet service was taken for granted—a sure indication of England's supremacy on the high seas.

The chief appeal of the letters though, lies in their delightful style, which has a purity and lightness of touch at once effortless, sincere—and fascinating. No matter what William Bragge is describing, a golden thread of humour runs through all his writing and he creates a graphic picture of the Peninsula in all its facets with a charm of rare quality. And as one follows the young officer—and his little bay mare—from Lisbon out across the hot, dusty plains of northern Spain to beyond the Pyrenees, he comes to life as a gay, witty personality of intellect and substance, who is always sustained by thoughts of his home and who possesses that infectious gift of making light of adversity.

In order to render the text more readable, I have revised the punctuation in places, especially where a full stop is more appropriate today than a nineteenth-century semi-colon, and I have given the modern version of geographical features and place names throughout. Apart from this, the spelling has not been amended—the few quaint words are quite recognizable—and I have preserved the capital letters at the beginning of particular words because this was the accepted method of emphasizing them. Notes on the text are set out at the end of the book, together with a section of biographical notes on persons mentioned in the Letters. Among the latter, the best known and those for whom long research would not be adequately rewarding have been omitted.

In assembling the material for this book, I have received much kind help from many quarters. I am particularly indebted to Commander W. J. Eyre for details on Sadborow and to Sir Denis Le Marchant for information on Major General John Le Marchant. In Portugal my thanks are due especially to Mrs. Lowndes Marques for certain local details and for the use of a quotation from *The Selective Traveller in Portugal* and to Coronel F. E. Baptista for locating material on Lieut. General Carlos Lecor.

I would like to record my thanks to the staff of the Public Records Office and of the Print Room of the British Museum. Finally my chief obligations are due to Professor C. C. Lloyd of the Royal Naval College, Greenwich, and Mr. Hector Bolitho for their encouragement, enthusiasm and helpful guidance throughout the preparation of this book.

London, June, 1963. S.A.C.C.

Prologue

Between Chard in Somerset and Lyme Bay, the river Blackwater flows quietly through a broad valley to join the Axe. Commanding the gentle rise on its northern side and looking out across the wide sweep to the ruins of Lambert's Castle and the Woodlands of Westhay on the skyline to the south, there stands a dignified Georgian house of mellow Dorset stone—Sadborow—which was the seat of the Bragge family from 1573 until 1933.

Sadborow has a long history, for there was mention of it in Saxon times and the Domesday Book also records a brief statement on it as one of the properties of the Earl of Devon. The estate came into the possession of the Bragges as a result of some complicated transactions following the Dissolution of the Monasteries, in which Sir Christopher Hatton and a William Churchill were also involved. During the next two centuries the family served their country and sovereign loyally, representing the County in Parliament and acting as High Sheriffs and Justices of the Peace. Not without incident, however. The Bragges supported the Royalists in the Civil War and on one occasion Sadborow was sacked by the Roundheads, 'who took store of silken gowns and scarlet clothes with much pillage'[1] in retaliation for failing to ambush the Squire and his troop. Sadborow survived while other properties were sequestrated or sold to pay the heavy fines of the Protectorate. When Monmouth landed at Lyme Regis, a cousin Matthew, it is said, had the misfortune to be seized and compelled to act as guide for a patrol one evening. The following morning his horse was stolen, so—it is briefly recorded—'he took his cane and gloves and walked home'.[2] An informer gave evidence and in spite of copious witnesses to prove his innocence, he was condemned to death by the ruthless Jeffries at Dorchester in September 1685.

In the eighteenth century the family was not beset by such occurrences, although at one time its continuation hung by a thread. John, the grandfather of the writer of these Letters, inherited Sadborow when he was eight years old and for eighteen years he was the only Bragge. When he married Elizabeth Adney—a lady of considerable beauty and fortune (she was painted by Gainsborough twice)—in 1762, the old manor house had fallen into a sad state of disrepair. It is said that she 'refused to live in a farmhouse'. Certainly she did not go to Sadborow until it had been rebuilt. The new house, which is attributed to Richard Johnston, better known for his works in Dublin, was completed on a site higher up the park in 1771.

The 'Bath Heiress'—as Elizabeth is generally known to the family—cannot but have admired her new home. The restrained interior by one of the rivals of the Adam brothers has particular grace and charm; a circular stone staircase with a slender wrought-iron balustrade, which rises under a cupola at the end of the wide entrance hall, and the simple beauty of the original ceiling decorations of the ground-floor rooms and above the staircase are especially attractive. Except for the addition of a Victorian front portico, the house stands today with its distinctive bay windows rising to the full height of three floors almost unchanged after nearly two centuries. Of the older building no trace remains.

Into these well-ordered surroundings and to this heritage, William, the eldest son of John and Anne Bragge was born on 5 June 1788, and here he grew up with his two brothers and two sisters, John, Champneys, Lucy and Charlotte. He was educated at Winchester and University College, Oxford, where he matriculated in December 1806 at the age of eighteen. These are the few recorded facts about his early years.

William was gazetted to a Cornetcy in the 3rd Dragoons on 24 May 1810. The exact circumstances which led to his joining the Regiment are not known. The family was on very good terms with Sir William Oglander of Parnham, near Beaminster, who was connected by marriage with General Lord Charles Fitzroy. The Fitzroys were associated with the 3rd Dragoons in several ways, so one suspects that his 'interest' lay there.

The 3rd Dragoons came into being in 1685 when five independent troops which had been raised hurriedly to stem Monmouth's uprising were subsequently integrated to form the Queen's Consort's Regiment of Dragoons. The Regiment was engaged at the Battle of the Boyne in 1690 and after its name had been changed to the King's Own Dragoons in 1714, fought with distinction at Sheriffmuir, Dettingen and Fontenoy. Following the Peninsular campaigns, the Regiment acquired further honours with an impressive record of service in India and in both World Wars. During this time a number of changes occurred; it was converted to a regiment of Light Dragoons shortly after Waterloo and later to a Hussar regiment, which in due course was mechanized. Finally in 1958 the Regiment was amalgamated with the 7th Hussars to form the Queen's Own Hussars.

On 10 November 1810 William was promoted Lieutenant. Until the following summer he was stationed with the Regiment at Guildford, at which time it is convenient to become more acquainted with his circumstances and follow him to the Peninsula.

B

CHAPTER ONE

Wimbledon Common to Ciudad Rodrigo

June 1811–January 1812

On 9 June 1811, the 3rd Dragoons mounted entirely on black horses for the last time, together with the Life Guards, 2nd Dragoon Guards, Foot Guards and many other regiments, were present for the Review of 20,000 cavalry and infantry by the Prince Regent before some 200,000 spectators on Wimbledon Common. The occasion was enthusiastically reported by *The Times* in a long article: 'The eager curiosity excited by the superb military spectacle... attracted thousands from the metropolis and the neighbouring counties.... The extent of the heath, the beauty of the day, the fineness of the different regiments, the steadiness of the discipline, the exactness of their manoeuvres and the assembled crowds reaching from one end of the Common to the other all made the spectacle such an one as can scarcely be described.'[1]

It was to be a memorable day for the 3rd Dragoons. As they passed the Prince Regent on his richly caparisoned charger (whose saddle it was said cost near 500 guineas), dispersed from the Common and rode down to Guildford, they were bound for sterner service. Although the Regiment had formed part of the ill-fated Walcheren expedition in 1809, there is no evidence that it ever disembarked, so over sixty years had passed since the whole Regiment had last fought in battle—at Fontenoy in 1745. Four more years were to elapse before it would again share in the glitter and pomp of military ceremony—in the presence of another monarch in a conquered capital.

During June and July preparations were being made for the impending departure of a heavy brigade of cavalry comprising the 4th and 5th Dragoon Guards and the 3rd Dragoons. The brigade was commanded by Major General Le Marchant, a most capable and accomplished officer. His plan for the establishment of a Royal Military Academy had led to the founding of a military College first at High Wycombe and also later at Great Marlow—in effect the forerunners of Camberley and Sandhurst respectively. He had been the first Lieutenant Governor of High Wycombe until he was appointed to command the Brigade. He was also a gifted water-colour painter and his pencil and paint brush were never idle for long. The 3rd Dragoons were under the command of Lieut. Colonel Mundy, a worthy but limited officer, whose enduring attributes were confined to marrying Admiral Lord Rodney's daughter and writing a biography of his father-in-law.

When the Regiment had been brought up to strength with a draft of a hundred extra horses, it embarked in three divisions at Portsmouth on 25, 26 and 27 July. William boarded his vessel on the first day with his three horses: his first charger—a dun mare—, his 'old brown horse' and his 'little bay mare', the last of which was destined to serve him so valiantly throughout his whole time in the Peninsula.

The previous two months had been a testing time for Lord Wellington. Masséna, 'stared out of countenance by that impenetrable blend of geography and fortification'[2] at Torres Vedras, had dragged the starving remnants of his army through the barren, wasted countryside to Salamanca in March and April. After an immense exertion he had managed to assemble a powerful force with which to lunge westwards once more. At Fuentes de Oñoro Lord Wellington had saved the north of Portugal but in the south, on 16 May—eleven days later—the bloody battle of Albuera had been fought and there had followed a critical week at the end of June when the Anglo-Portuguese army had faced a numerically superior concentration of Marshals Soult and Marmont (who had succeeded Masséna), united for the relief of Badajoz. By the end of the month, however, Soult had hurried away to his province of Andalusia, where resistance had hardened uncomfortably during his absence. Marmont followed his example a fortnight later, retiring northwards to the Tagus with his Army of Portugal, after Badajoz had been revictualled with six months' supplies. The danger of a fourth invasion of Portugal had passed.

Although the immediate recovery of Badajoz, the southern gateway to Spain, had been denied to Lord Wellington, he could be thankful of being able to quit the blistering heat and dreaded fevers of the Guadiana valley. As soon as it was safe to do so, the Allied army was on the move as well. Leaving the 2nd Division, a Portugese infantry brigade and some cavalry under the competent command of General Hill to cover the fortress of Elvas, the rest of the army was marched off to regain its health and strength for a short while in the more salubrious villages between Portalegre and Castelo Branco.

When the transports bringing the 3rd Dragoons to the Peninsula sailed up the Tagus at the end of August, the Army was once more back in its familiar ground between the Coa and Agueda rivers, threatening Ciudad Rodrigo with the help of Spanish Guerillas. As the Regiment disembarked at Lisbon and marched to its quarters at Belem, Lord Wellington was writing to Lord Liverpool, the Secretary for War: 'An augmentation of cavalry will give us great advantages. . . . I am therefore very glad that you have sent Le Marchant's Brigade.' In addition, knowing Marmont's supply difficulties from two intercepted letters, he was able to conclude guardedly from the results of the recent arduous campaigning: 'We have certainly altered the nature of the war in Spain; it has become to a certain degree offensive on our part.'[3] It was an auspicious moment to arrive.

Five days after William landed in Portugal, he wrote to his father describing his first impressions and the prospects before him.

No. 1.   Belem,
                                                     August 29th 1811.

My Dear Father,

The last Packet for England sailed on the 24th, the Day we arrived and as I lost that opportunity of writing, you will have heard of our safe arrival one week before you receive this. The said Packets sail Weekly and a Letter directed to me, Post Paid, and the Name of the Reg^t given, will be speedily forwarded to any Part of Portugal or Spain.

Another Convoy, with the 5th Dragoon Guards on board came into the River Yesterday but will I believe not turn us out for a Day or two, our Horses being all tender Footed and many Bare of Shoes. Whenever we leave this Town we shall probably proceed towards Ld Wellington's Army which I understand is a Month's March over the worst Roads in Europe, but with regard to any News of him or his Army you will at present derive more correct Information from the Newspapers than from me, having scarcely heard his name mentioned.

After leaving Plymouth our Passage to Lisbon was a very quick one, being only 10 Days out of which we had 2 compleat blanks. I saw two Whales spouting Water close to the Vessel, a Number of large Sharks and Multitudes of Poirpoise, whose clumsy sport in the Water is truly laughable. Sea and Sky, Sky

and Sea were the only objects to look at during the Days these
Watery Monsters remained below and as reading and writing is
not easily managed by a Landsman at Sea, I found the Voyage
tedious, tho' never sick or the least unwell.

The entrance to Lisbon is truly grand and Beautiful, it being
built on Seven Hills rising from the Water's edge and every
Building retaining its original colour of White. Here ends the
Beauty of Lisbon for on setting your Foot on Land you are
almost overcome with the Stench, every Filth being thrown
into the Street and there left until it pleases God to wash the
Town with a Shower of Rain, a rare occurrence except at particular Seasons of the Year, when I hear they are deluged with it.
The Inhabitants all have an unhealthy appearance, an immense
proportion of them Blind and objects of the most distressing
Kind are met with in every corner—in short such miserable
sights I never before witnessed nor will you and my Mother
readily believe the dreadful Accounts I hope one Day or other
to give you of the wretched Natives of Portugal, where the
Virtues of old Cuming's Ancestor are clearly depicted in every
Portuguese Countenance.

Dreading to enter any House the first night, I gladly accepted
a Bed on the Floor of an Englishman's House where two other
Officers were accommodated in the same Way. I accordingly
turned in and then underwent the severest Pennance Fleas &
Bugs can inflict; and as long as I live the first bed in Portugal
will be remembered. I now sleep at a House where the People
are extremely civil and for Portuguese very neat—no Vermin
or Mosquitoes in the House. These latter gentry have as yet
kept clear of me and I trust I am one of the favoured few not to
be molested by these Devils who have stung most of the Officers
until they have the Appearance of Men after an inocculation
for the Small Pox.

There are many Superb Buildings in Lisbon but the only
ones I have yet visited are the Prince's Riding House and Stables,
the latter of which have Marble Mangers with reservoirs of
Water at each end and could contain under one Roof two hundred more Horses than we have now got in them. There are no
Stalls or racks and I fear many Horses will get badly kicked; we
lost 18 in the Passage.[4, 5]

Mine are yet well but the Bay Mare does everything in her

Power to lame the others. She is to be the second Charger and
the old brown Horse my Mule, who will have to carry a Pair of
Saddle Bags about half full containing my Kit and my Serv^ts
with two Blankets and a Tent which I have undertaken to carry
if the Captain [Jacson] will bring on the Canteens and Prog.

Two things particularly amuse me here, the Carriages and
Life Guards, the latter of which are fine looking Men mounted
on wretched Horses, the best the country will afford, whilst a
still inferior Species of Cattle draw their Charriots, driven
usually Post with a Pair of Shafts and an outrigger, the coach-
man mounted on a Wooden Saddle with Stirrups of the same
Metal made like coal Scuttles and always with a large cocked
Hat, the fashionable Beaver of the Country—and on Hot days
they throw an immense Cloak over the rest of their Clothes.

Rheumatism and Diarheas are the usual complaints of the
country but I trust by living temperately, wearing Flannels and
avoiding Fruit to escape two Disorders which have already
carried off Numbers.

I make no bones of Strutting into a Shop or Coffee House and
calling for things in Portuguese and rarely miss making myself
understood. I expect Shortly to speak it tolerably well.

Hoping one day or other to return safe and sound to find you
all in health, I remain Your dutiful Son, WILLIAM BRAGGE.

N.B.   31st August 1811.

I never intended sending this to England but I sweat so pro-
fusely with writing Adney [his brother-in-law, married to his
sister Lucy] a Letter that I am absolutely compelled to change
my Things. We know nothing of our destination but have good
Reason to expect a Route for Evora, Vila Viçosa or some other
Place near Elvas there to await orders from Ld Wellington, who
is now besieging Ciudad Rodrigo. Many of our Officers are ill
in consequence of fancying themselves in England but I still
continue perfectly well and I understand this free Perspiration
is the likeliest Thing to keep me so. 500 Officers and 5,000
Soldiers wounded and sick have been embarked at Santarem
to come down the River within these last six Weeks, a pretty
prospect this is for us.

If my Mother's remedy for Agues is composed of Drugs

likely to be found in a Military Medicine Chest, do send it me
in your first Letter as Agues are prevalent in this country.

God Bless you all.

[On cover: LISBON SE 9 1811]

On 1 September there were over 12,000 British sick in the Allied
army. Little wonder that William was alarmed and most anxious
not to succumb to the local maladies.

While Le Marchant's brigade was still assembling at Lisbon—the
4th Dragoon Guards had preceded the 3rd Dragoons fiom England
but the 5th Dragoon Guards, who had left Portsmouth on 12 August,
were only just entering the Tagus—William wrote again, still
bitterly conscious of the dreadful conditions he had to endure.

At Le Marchant's inspection of the Regiment there were twenty
officers, 548 N.C.O.s and men and 518 troop horses.

No. 2.   Belem,
                                                        Septr 6th 1811.

My Dear Father,

As my old Schoolfellow Gore Langton is about to return to
England by the next Packet I shall not neglect so favourable
an opportunity of informing you I had on the 6th of Sept^r
passed a Fortnight in this wretched country without suffering
any material inconvenience either from intense Heat or extreme
Filth of Lisbon and its Vicinity, where the front of every House
is garnished with just such a Puddle as you, in your Afternoon's
Walk, will find before Isaac Hawker's Cottage in the Road to
Hew Wood. Here it is regularly replenished at Nine O' Clock at
Night to the great annoyance of the unwary Traveller. Most of
our Officers have been indisposed and our sick Report at this
Morning's Parade amounted to Fifty Two Men unfit for Duty,
and as their Monthly Acc^{ts} are to be settled Tomorrow, I expect
as many more ill within these two Days.

General Le Marchant who commands the Brigade inspects
the Regiment Tomorrow Morning and I suppose in a Day or
two we shall take up the Quarters of the 4th Dragoon Guards
at Sacavem, they having received a Route to march to Abrantes.

Sacavem is about two Leagues from hence and by our marching there these quarters would be open for the 5th, who must have had a very long Passage as they were to quit Portsmouth immediately after us.

We hear little or nothing of Ld Wellington, who keeps not only the Portuguese but the Officers of his Staff in the dark with regard to his Intentions, and I understand at his own Table he rattles away to the General Officers etc., and fills them full of Humbug Accounts which they have scarce Time to repeat to their confidential Friends before an order arrives for the Brigades to march without Delay at least 20 Points of the Compass from the one expected. I saw a Letter from the Brigade Major of the Royals which says the Horses have been 6 Days without corn and another Regiment 13 Days, both were consequently obliged to fall back. He likewise mentions the 11th Reg^t having lost two Picquets and an odd file or two, which has so enraged Ld W. that he is determined to exchange the Officers immediately for the Purpose of bringing them to a Court Martial.

As I can give you no Accounts of the Army at large, you must be contented with a little news of some of your Acquaintances. In the first Place no one stands Shot and Shell with greater Phlegm than General Slade and I hear he was in conversation with Col. Hervey when a spent Shot struck the latter's Sabretache, which together with the Shot and a Volume of 'Tristram Shandy' lodged in the Horse's side and was afterwards cut out, Col. H. having received no injury but the loss of his Horse and a slight Bruise on his own Leg.[6] Genl Hawker is coming Home to take command of the Southampton District, having been disappointed in endeavouring to obtain a Brigade here and Sir G. Calcraft ranks amongst the first Cavalry Officers in this country. I have no doubt these form but a slight portion of your acquaintance in this Part of the World but I have heard of no others yet except Officers of the 11th, amongst whom Col. Cumming is so troublesome that Diggens and several others have entered the Portuguese Service.

Saturday 7th.

Last Night we heard of another Party of the Eleventh consisting of a Serg^t, 2 Corporals and twelve Privates being surprised and taken by the French, making the Third Picquet they have lost;[7] and as no Man or Officer of this Reg[t] has ever been on Duty near the Enemy's Post, I fear some of us will share the same Fate ere long. The General inspected us this Morning and immediately reported our being in a proper State to march up to the Army, therefore I trust we shall remain here but a few Days longer as every Thing is as dear as in London and nothing half so good. Rice, Sugar and Coffee are to be procured in most of the Villages but as for any Thing else, it is not to be bought at any Price. I likewise hear we shall never see a Bed again after leaving Lisbon.

People are fond of saying that the Portuguese are partial to us, but at the same Time caution us against leaving a Single Article without a Guard as the Natives up the Country make no Bones of marching out of a Stable with Arms, Accoutrements or any Thing else belonging to the English; indeed at Abrantes they stole Four Troop Horses from the Twelfth. I am now going into Lisbon to buy a Hammock as I foolishly left England with out a Bear Skin [rug]. Whenever an opportunity offers I shall not neglect writing to you and shall now put this in the Post as Langton appears undetirmined about going.

Give my Love to my Mother, Brothers and Sisters and believe me, Your dutiful Son, WILLIAM BRAGGE.

[On cover: LISBON SE 9 1811]

The Regiment's protracted stay at Belem was evidently straining William's purse. In his next letter he had to broach the problem of lack of funds.

No. 3.   Belem,
                                                    Sept[r] 14th 1811.
My Dear Father,

As the probability of our remaining at Belem is greatly increased by the arrival of the Fifth Dragoon Guards, the return of our General to England[8] and a great Scarcity of Forage in the country, I find that Necessity will compel me to draw on you for some Money which I intend doing in a way not sanctioned by you, but which I trust, when you consider my present situation, and the difficulty of procuring it in any other way without paying a most exhorbitant discount, you will readily pardon, and by a Timely Notice save my credit with an English

Merchant, your Banker, and what is of more consequence to me, with my Friend Heywood through whose interest I shall obtain from a Mr Sealy in Lisbon 30£ or 40£ by giving him a draft on your Banker, payable at 14 days Sight.

I am perfectly aware of the Impropriety of this proceeding which I should not have recoursed to, were there a Probability of hearing from you in a week or a Fortnight but as 6 Weeks may elapse before I can procure an Answer, I shall get the Money from him in the course of the Week and rely on your usual generous Indulgence.

I have acquainted both Sealy (who is the greatest Merchant in the Place) and Heywood, that you had allowed me to draw on you but Mr S. wished for a draft on London as he had no connection with any People living in the County, therefore I have only to desire you to suffer my draft on its being presented to be accepted by Batson, who I have heard you say is remarkably particular.

Except for a few fits of the King Agrippa I have continued in as good health as ever, tho' I fear it will not be long before I shall suffer from this Climate which has not failed to attack most of my Acquaintance in some way or other, and at this moment our Sick List is more than double what it was when I last wrote to you. I have heard from good Authority that the Deaths in our Hospitals here and at Lisbon have for some Time averaged more than Seventy a Week.[9]

By the latest accounts from Ld Wellington's Army, we heard that he was still waiting in the Vicinity of Ciudad Rodrigo for his Battering Train which was then about 100 Miles from him on the Road from Oporto, drawn by 500 Oxen and advancing at a rate of 8 or 10 Miles a Day,[10] but as this Town is still stronger than Badajoz, I believe there are but slight Hopes of its surrendering to the English, and our Politicians in the Country suppose that the Alentejo will for many reasons be the seat of war before long as it is the Weakest Part of the Country, is near Lisbon, and has hitherto escaped the Ravages of the French. Blake has again been defeated with immense loss, but as most of my Intelligence is derived from Col. Mundy, I shall not give you any more Reports as the little Man deals them out with little or no Authority and had the other Day reinforced the French with 60,000 Men.[11]

The English have ruined this Market as they do all others, and at this moment every Thing from a Hen's Egg to a Mule is dearer than in England. A Poney, smaller than the one you bought at White down, is sold for 50 or 60 Dollars.

They appear to have no Manufactories or any means of working Iron but by the Hammer; in short it appears like a Nation supported in every necessary and convenience by England, to whom they are indebted for every individual Utensil either for the Kitchen or Table.

Their mode of Shoeing a Horse is particularly astonishing to me as the whole Foot is rendered insensible by the Practise of cutting out the Frog and hammering the Shoe on with immense Nails all round the Toe, notwithstanding which they have few lame Horses or Broken Knees. The Ladies and Gentlemen bathe together and our watching them is considered a high compliment, and as few of them can read, write, work or draw, the Gentleman ammuses himself with a few hours sleep in the day Time, whilst his Wife and Daughters sit in the Parlour Windows and amuse themselves with searching each others Heads, a Chase which seldom fails affording considerable sport to its Amateurs.

I rode out a few Miles into the country once in order to have a sight of their magnificent Aqueduct which reaches 16 Miles in length and has some Arches 300 Feet high, but the roads are so dreadfully Bad that I do not think I shall be tempted to ride again for Pleasure.

Traitors and Murderers are some of them handled roughly here, one is Ham strung and chained to a Bed of Flints, whilst the Murderer . . . is beheaded and his Head and Hands [and Feet stuck on a Pole,] a specimen of which may now [be seen] by the British Envoy's House between this and Lisbon.

I have bought a Hammock, the produce of Chard Manufactory and had travelled to Lisbon before I knew sail Cloth was made there.

A Packet arrived this Morning by which I received no Letters, but as Five are still due I hope to hear from you in a Day or two.

It rained Yesterday for the first Time since 20th June, so you may suppose how green the Fields are—in short the whole country at this Time appears like one continual Bed of Flints.

Do tell Farmer Fowler the Oxen are here 16 Hands high and draw almost entirely by the Horns which is absolutely true, and I think in this and this only the Inhabitants can give the English a Lesson. Be kind enough to give my love to my Mother, Brothers, and Sisters if at Home and believe me, Your dutiful Son, WILLIAM BRAGGE.

P.S.

This Letter must have a week's start of my Draft and should it not arrive first I trust Mr Batson would write you word of my having drawn on him.

This Portuguese Paper is so Thin and damp, that I fear it will rub through unless I put a cover on it. I wish you to observe that the day when the Letter was put into the Office will be seen with the Direction.

W.B.

[On Cover: MISSENT to LONDON]

Owing to the irregular manner in which the Army was paid and to the monstrously high interest demanded by the Lisbon money lenders, William was compelled, like most other officers, to obtain money by private means. In spite of his arrangement with Mr Sealy, his finances were to become even more involved. They were not properly solved for over a year.

The Regiment remained at Belem until 19 September, when the three squadrons left on consecutive days to march up country. William reached Abrantes on the 27th, from where he described the march, still very apprehensive of the disgusting beds and the alarming sickness which had begun to take its toll of the 3rd Dragoons.

No. 4.   [Abrantes,
                                                          28th Septr 1811.]

[My Dear Father,]

On the 17th September we received an unexpected order to march by Sqds from Lisbon to this Place where we arrived Yesterday after having passed through Vila Franca, Santarem and other Places rendered particularly interesting at this Time from having so lately been the seat of War. We have been fortunate in our Weather and upon the whole have had a most delightful march through the only part of the country worth seeing, and can now form a pretty correct Idea of the miseries of War. We found whole Villages without an Inhabitant and

Towns, which were two Years ago in the utmost Prosperity, are now the residence of a few wretched Inhabitants whose countenances betray the greatest Misery. At Santarem 11 Convents and 8 Churches fell a Victim to the French, who have been guilty of the most wanton Mischief, such as tearing down Altar Pieces and Tombs so perfectly useless to them that at this Moment these relicks of former magnificence are remaining in the Body of the church, mutilated and destroyed, with one solitary Workman to repair Damages that would at least require 100 Men the next 5 Years. Santarem is beautiful beyond description and is remarkable in my Journal for the Quantity of Business I did in my Shirt and for having been the Place where I first caught a Louse on Service.

I now regret having come from England without a Bearskin [rug] as the Portuguese Beds are so full of Fleas that I cannot possibly Sleep in them and am usually compelled to quit my Post before Twelve and pass the remainder of the night on the Chair. I have a Hammock with me but fear it is too clumsy to swing in a Tent.

I have not received a Letter from you yet but expect to hear from you by the next Packet. I understand that Letters for Portugal should be in London on Wednesday Night, in order to be in Time for the Vessel which regularly sails from Falmouth on a Saturday, and I should be obliged to you to get *Bell's Weekly Magazine* or some other Newspaper sent out as our Regiment have wisely forgot to order any.

In my last Letter I wrote you word of my intending to borrow Money of Mr Sealy and giving him a Draft on your Banker for the amount. He advanced me 100 Dollars and would then neither receive a Draft or Receipt, assuring me I should require more, and that at any time I might give him one, but as life is short and I may never see him again I shall enclose him a Draft on you for thirty Pounds which he will most likely keep as a receipt, but should it arrive in England I would thank you to pay it.

Our Men have been extremely ill and I am sorry to say still continue falling sick of the Flux, but many have been completely cured by our giving them Dr Moncrieffe's Proscription and I am now going to purchase all the Tinct of Rhubarb in the Town, which will scarcely fill a Half Pint Bottle.[12]

Our March has for three Days been along the Banks of the Tagus where the Views are so very beautiful and Picturesque that I really dreaded some of the Men riding over the Precipeces which are badly fenced off. The Roads are very Bad but nothing like what we had reason to expect from the very exaggerated Accts which were given us, though I cannot say that a Pack of Fox Hounds which were brought on Shore at Belem would be any great acquisition in any part of the country we have passed through. The Orange Groves and Vineyards are at present scarcely worth seeing as the Grapes are gathered and the Oranges not ripe.

Except a little touch of the Flux at Santarem I have continued quite well as have all my Horses, and as long as that is the Case I have little to care about. We have no orders to proceed at present but expect in a Day or two to move on towards Fuente Guinaldo, the present HeadQuarters of the Army, but even at this distance we hear not the slightest News from thence.

I hope my Mother and all the Family are well. Be good enough to give my Love to them and believe me, Your dutiful Son, WILLIAM BRAGGE.

William's next letter was written just before the Regiment marched out of Abrantes, where it had been quartered for about three weeks.

Col. Mundy had fallen sick the first day out from Belem and the Regiment was temporarily commanded by Major Clowes. Fleas were the torment of the whole Army. One young officer was so plagued that he committed suicide.

At the end of September Wellington had withdrawn to his carefully prepared defensive positions by Sabugal after the spirited action at El Bodon, where the 11th Lt. Dragoons and the 1st Hussars, King's German Legion, distinguished themselves.

No. 5.   Abrantes,
                                                          October 13th 1811.

My Dear Father,

The Probability of hearing from you together with the uncertainty of our future destination for the Winter has induced me to delay writing to you until this Morning, when an order arrived for us to march immediately to Castelo Branco, a Town

much nearer the Army, and in most respects a more desirable
Winter Quarter than Abrantes, which is remarkably unhealthy
although situated on a Lofty Hill close to the River Tagus.

I hope in the course of a few Weeks to receive Letters from
England constantly, but as Information of our arrival had not
appeared in the London Prints so late as the 12th of September,
I am but slightly disappointed at not hearing from you yet.

I live with Jacson (who commands the Troop I am attached
to) and Major Clowes who has command of the Regiment, and
have consequently felt no inconvenience from being on Service
except from the utter impossibility of sleeping in any Portuguese Bed, the whole of which are most abundantly stocked
with a Race of Fleas more venomous and hungry than any to be
met with in England. These Devils attack me instantly and in
about 10 Minutes dislodge me for the Night, but as there is
neither Bed, Bedstead, or Bedclothes North of this Place I shall
have no Bait laid for me again. At present I sleep on an old
Chest about 4 Feet long and make up a Bed with Two Blankets
and a Cloak. On this downy couch I usually sleep from ½ past
seven in the Evening until the Morning when we all get up and
walk down the Mountain and back which is sufficient exercise
for the Day.

We hear a great deal about the abundance of game in this
country but have never succeeded in finding more than one
Brace of Partridges in a Morning.

When reading *Guthrie's Grammar*[13] at Home, I often wished
to see the Orange and Olive Groves, Vineyards and Cork Trees
etc., of Portugal but having now marched through every variety
of Scenery which this Country affords, I care not how soon the
Campaign is over and I and my Guthrie once more in the
Parlour at Sadborow.

I have this Morning seen a Letter from an Officer of Ld
Wellington's Staff who gives a miserable Account of their
Quarters and indeed of the Army itself, the Sickness of which
continues to be excessive.[14] He likewise adds that a liberal supply
of Money which the Inhabitants in that Quarter are to receive
immediately will scarcely save them from Starving. Some part
of our own People (I believe the 4th Drgs) received no Bread for 48
Hours and Forage is so scarce that they are forced to carry every
sack of Corn from this Magazine.

I trust that Colonel Mundy will return to England as he is himself no Officer and must take the Command out of excellent Hands whenever he arrives at the Regiment. Our Men have been very sickly but nothing in comparison with the 4th Dragoon Guards who arrived about 8 Days before us and have at this Moment 189 Men unfit for Duty. In consequence of this they have given up a Number of Horses to the Royals which I hope we shall escape from doing.[15]

News from the Army is always on the High Seas before a Rumour of it is spread in Abrantes, therefore you must have seen an Account of the Brilliant Conduct of the 11th Dragoons and 1st [German] Hussars who, I believe, charged an immense Cavalry Force any number of Times from 7 to 16, which together with the Circumstances of 2 of our Regiments of Infantry (by no means strong ones) frequently repelling and ultimately charging Cavalry meant to charge them, has been deservedly applauded by Ld Wellington in his General Orders.[16]

General Le Marchant marched part of the Way hither with our Squadron and regularly treated us with dinners. He is a pleasant Man, highly accomplished and a great Theoretical Warrior, but I greatly fear we shall in him experience how very much Practise exceeds Theory.

Most of the Articles of Housekeeping are much dearer than in England as you will see from a short Acct of Market Prices— Wine 5s 6d, Brandy 6d, and Porter 3d a Bottle. Tea is as high as 1s 5d, Cheese 2s 6d, and butter 2s 3d per lb. After this you will be surprised to hear that a full sized Sheep can be bought for 8s 9d, but as the said Animal cuts up into Quarters of 3 lb. Weight, I doubt whether it is much cheaper than Butcher's meat in England. We eat our Rations and drink the Wine, the latter of which is in this Store very fair Tipple.

With regard to eating or drinking there is, I believe, not a single Thing which some kind adviser has not recommended us to avoid, stating that his own illness was occasioned by it. We have even been warned against the Pernicious Custom of eating Soups and Broth, while others have as strenuously opposed wearing Flannel or drinking Wine, but I rather think the Line of conduct we shall adopt is one recommended by Colonel Charles Egerton of Cheshire: 'At all Times, and in all Places, live as well as you possibly can.' The cause of this Variety of Opinion

II. Lisbon and the Aqueduct of Alcantara.
From an engraving of 1809.

III. The Pontoon Bridge at Vila Velha.

is that scarcely any Constitution can stand the Climate and every one attributes his illness to the last thing he happened to eat.

The Portuguese are, I believe, notorious for being more superstitious than Religious but in this Town their Idolatory exceeds everything you can possibly imagine as every Cross, Church, Painted Pan Tile or Fountain receives some mark of Respect and usually a bit of a Prayer from every Individual who passes. The Women drop a Courtesey and the Gentlemen make one of their lowest Bows and pull off their Hats. We have a miserable daub of our Saviour opposite the Window, which is regularly treated with a Lamp every night by the People of the House, and we as regularly see a Mouse pay his Devoirs to the Oil, the whole of which is commonly devoured before Midnight.

This Language bears a very great Affinity to the Latin and is likewise so much like the Spanish that I hope with the Assistance of some Friar at Castelo Branco to be pretty Proficient in both Languages before the Winter is over.

We hear from all Quarters that the Next Campaign is to be a brilliant one and that Ld Wellington with his present Strength of Cavalry (15 Reg^{ts}) intends forcing the French at all Quarters, instead of acting on the Defensive only, which I sincerely hope may be the case, and that one campaign may put an end to a War, which most People expect will last as long as Bounaparte lives.

As I was obliged to leave Lisbon without giving Mr Sealy a Draft, I sent him one from this Place dated 1st October. It is for 30£, drawn on you and payable at 10 Days sight. I wish I could have avoided it but our stay in Lisbon was so long and Pay so uncertain that it was impossible.

Remember me kindly to my Mother, Brothers and Sisters and believe me, Your dutiful Son, WILLIAM BRAGGE.

P.S.

Did I caution you to pay the Postage of Letters for Portugal? Tell Mrs Egerton [the wife of the Vicar of Thorncombe, the Parish of Sadborow] that the 29th Reg^t are on their return to England and will I believe bring a Nephew of hers with them. My Horses are all well and two of them very fat.

[On Cover: Rec^d Nov. 2nd, answered in London Nov. 6.]

c

Four days later the 3rd Dragoons reached Castelo Branco, having passed through Gavião and Niza and having crossed the Tagus by the pontoon bridge at Vila Velha. The Regiment remained in the town for the rest of the year.

The number of sick in the Regiment had been rising steadily. Fifty-six men had been left at Belem in addition to Col. Mundy. There were eighty-nine in hospital by the end of October.

Gen. Hill had surprised and routed the greater part of a French division under Girard as it was assembling in Arroyo Molinos during the early hours of 28 September.

William wrote from Castelo Branco...

No. 6.   Castelo Branco,
                                                       First Novr 1811.

My Dear Father,

We marched into this Town on the 19th October from Abrantes and have every Reason to expect it will be our Winter Quarters during this rainy season, which has already commenced with considerable Violence and will probably continue with little Intermission until the latter end of February, when I trust the King's Own will take the Field with more effective Men and Horses than any Regiment in the Country.

At present we have scarcely one effective Man to two Horses, but as our convalescents amount to nearly one Hundred and this is considered the most salubrious Season of the Year, I hope to give a better Account of ourselves in my next Letter. Colonel Mundy was taken ill of a Flux the day after we left Belem, which has reduced him to such a Degree that a Board of Medical Officers have ordered him to England without delay. He commenced his Letter informing Major Clowes of this Circumstance with 'My Doom is fixed' but as he is Father of six Infant Children and in daily Expectation of another, I cannot give him credit for so much grief, especially as his commission forms the principal part of a small Fortune.

I received your Letter on the 19th and was extremely happy to find that you and all the Family were well. Be good enough to inform my Mother that I consider her trusting me with so important a Secret a mark of particular Favour and shall not fail trying the experiment as soon as I can find a proper Subject, tho' there will be considerable difficulty in procuring the Ingredients in a country where Snuffers are unknown and candles rarely used. You may at that same time inform her Ladyship a Dragoon had observed the Day before I received your Letter, that more people were cured of the Ague at Canterbury by an old Woman (who administered *Gin* and *Snuff* of *Candle*) than by all the Medical Staff.

You may suppose this disorder is pretty prevalent as I see by the Morning Report 11 out of 30 Patients are at this Time affected with it.

We yesterday heard of General Hill's success but till within these 3 days never knew of his having left Portalegre, although we halted for 2 Days a short distance from it. The Officer who went through Castelo Branco had himself counted 1,000 Prisoners, amongst whom were a German Prince (I believe, Darenburgh) and one General Officer. The Business was well conducted and will be a good Haul for the Infantry and Cavalry.[17]

The late Governor of Ciudad Rodrigo halted here for a few Days. He is considered a clever Man and is certainly delighted with the Idea of seeing England, for which purpose I believe he became a Prisoner. He was taken by the Spanish Guerillas, a Cohort who carry on the most destructive War against the French and rarely pass a Day without killing some of them.[18] The General says they have no communication with the Spaniards and dare not go out Foraging without a Brigade of Infantry and Reg^t of Cavalry, that he has himself been three Years in the Country without news from any of his Friends in France, and that a *Moniteur* is never seen by any Officer except some of the leading People who, for their own sakes, keep the Events of the Time a profound secret. I know a Frenchman will say anything but at the same time believe a good deal of this Intelligence.

A Baker of this Town has lately returned from HeadQuarters without obtaining his End, which was the small Sum of 50,000 Crowns—this event has alarmed some of the Natives and I greatly fear we shall be put on Biscuit in consequence, which is rather provoking as the Bread is remarkably good.

This Nation in all the Arts, Sciences and comforts of this Life is many hundred Years behind the rest of the world, and at this moment have scarcely one house in a Thousand with Glass windows and not so great a Proportion with any Chimnies except the Kitchen, so that they have the pleasing alternative of sitting by Lamp Light or being blown out of the Window for at least 3 Months per Annum.

General Le Marchant intends taking up his Quarters with this Regᵗ, which will be a good thing for the Subalterns and indeed for the whole Concern. His Brigade Major is one of our own Captains, and Gabriel of the Bays with Lᵈ Euston [are] his Aid de camps.

We are forced to go 3 Leagues (12 miles) daily for Forage, which is I understand less than any Regiment farther in advance. Only calculate the Expence of Transportation in this Country at 200 Mules [for] each Cavalry Regᵗ at 1 Dollar a Day, a Captain to each forty Mules at 2 Dollars a Day, and both Man and Beast at the same Rations with Dragoons. The Muleteers are rationed only but I should suppose there are not less than 40 to a Regᵗ.

In consequence of Roberts not producing the Shooting Jacket, I have appointed another Store Keeper, as a hard family and harder Winter might otherwise reduce my Stock.

I conclude Adney and Lucy have quitted Sadborow by this Time. I have not heard from the Latter yet but expect one of the two Packets which are due will bring me Letters from her and yourself.

I have seen Newspapers as late as the 20ᵗʰ Sept. in which they speak of a comet, to be seen between such and such Hours. At that Time the Animal was conspicuous for the whole Night in this Country and had a most brilliant Tail.[19] I sent to you for a Newspaper before, of course a Weekly one—

I don't know a better Sign of the Army going into Winter Quarters than 4 Cars going to HeadQuarters with Wine, Hams and Stoves—this I saw Yesterday.

Be kind enough to give my Love to all and believe me your dutiful Son, WILLIAM BRAGGE.

P.S.

I trust the Time will come when I shall return to England a more perfect John Bull than even Adney himself.

During the march hither we were forced to bivouac on the Banks of the Tagus. It was my first Night of sleeping in a Tent and I wish it may be the last.

On 7 December, the Regiment was reviewed by Lieut. Gen. Sir Stapleton Cotton, the Commander of all the British Cavalry. He was thirty-eight years old, handsome, dashing, and never more richly dressed and accoutred than when in action. One senior officer was once heard to remark: 'What a valuable prize Sir Stapleton would be to the enemy; for that, taking him and his horse as they stood, he could not be worth less than five hundred pounds.'[20]

William's impressions of this colourful personality or of the review are not recorded for a letter written at Christmas never reached his father.

He wrote again on New Year's Day 1812, the day on which the orders for the attack on the fortress of Ciudad Rodrigo were issued.

No. 7.   Castelo Branco,
                                                     Jan^{ry} 1st 1812.

My Dear Father,

As it has happened that the New Year's Day should be the Day to writing English Letters, I cannot do better than give you a circumstantial account of the numerous reports which have been in circulation at Castelo Branco during the past Week, some of which will perhaps in the course of the next Year be brought about, but should they on the contrary prove quite the reverse, this Letter may perhaps occasion a laugh, when I and my comrades in Arms are leathered back to the Place from whence we came.

To begin with Lord Wellington's Army. It is currently reported that he has expressed himself better pleased with the late Exertions of the Spaniards than he has ever been since the commencement of the war, and it is farther stated that he believes an account of Genl Blake having compelled Suchet to raise the Siege of Valencia.[21] The Lord himself had on the 28th Decr put all cars etc., in Requisition for the purpose of conveying Fascines Gabions etc., to commence the Siege of Ciudad Rodrigo.[22] This News I get from a Colonel's Letter of the 37th, who farther states that our own Army in that Neighbourhood had already been nearly one Month on half Rations of Biscuit.

General Hill has again advanced his Division into Spain and was on the 25th of December at Alburquerque accompanied by an immense proportion of commissariat Mules. This far I am

certain, but whether his Intention is merely to cut off the com-
munication between the French Army and the Garrison of
Badajoz or to attack a weak Division left in protection of some
Artillery in that Quarter is a Peg too high for my Information.[23]
With regard to Badajoz itself, I believe there is not the slightest
doubt of great disturbances having taken Place between the
French and Polish Soldiers, which may be attended with the
best consequences.[24]

The French have likewise retired from the Towns on this
Frontier and the Portuguese General Lecor (who procures most
excellent Intelligence) informs us that Marmont's Rear Guard
is now at Toledo. The General likewise asserts that the whole
of the Imperial Guards have quitted Spain.[25] Thus have I gleaned
from a Portuguese General, a wandering Scotch Major, a few
Letters [and] a number of Reports, all favourable to the cause;
and should I in the course of the next twelve Months be enabled
to confirm them I shall not consider our Time in the Peninsula
at all ill spent.

Yours of the Ninth of Decr I received on the 29th and was
extremely happy to hear so good an account of all at Home. I
was likewise glad to find you had paid Mr Sealy's Draft for me
especially as I have been endeavouring to procure some more
Money from the same Quarter, but I begin to fear the Drafts
I sent him have miscarried as I can neither hear from him or
the Person I desired to forward me the Dollars, and there is, I
fear, little probability of our receiving any part of our Pay for
this next Month, notwithstanding immense quantities of Dollars [which] are continually passing through this Place to the
Paymaster General. 50 Mules came in Yesterday and as many
more will arrive Tomorrow.

I have at length accomplished a Bedstead on the principle of
a Camp Stool, which stands nearly 2 feet from the Ground, is
quite Firm and only weighs about 30 lbs.

I should be very glad to hear you had converted the chestnut
Horse into a Specie as I am convinced he must be a useless Brute
to you—indeed I don't know what you have that is of use except
Old Major.

We have for some Time past entertained considerable fears
for our Colonel, who I am happy to say has at length arrived
safe in England together with about 20 Men unable to stand

the Climate. We have likewise sent home two out of five Q^r Masters.[26]

The Weather this Day, yesterday, and indeed for this last week has been I should conceive many Degrees colder than in England and the Serra da Estrêla, which we see from hence, is completely covered with Snow. I could not have believed this when we first landed. The rainy Season has not yet commenced but we may be in daily expectation of this dreary Time—I am at this Moment not worth half a Dollar, notwithstanding which I this morning purchased a Horse which upon a more minute Examination proved to be a Spanish Stallion.

With love to all and wishing you many returns of the Season, I remain My dear Father, Your dutiful Son, WILLIAM BRAGGE.

P.S.

I may well say that in Ars scribendi I follow you . . . . but I very much doubt I shall be the second best of the Family as I have only received two shabby Postscripts from Lucy. I have not heard from Jack this Twelvemonth and I am not certain that either Charlotte or Champ can write, never having seen a Letter from either.

[On Cover: LISBON JA 22 1812]

William wrote again eight days later, happy to have some money at last.

The *Weekly Messenger* of John Bell (1745–1831) was well regarded for its country news. Maj. Gen. Auchmuty with 3,500 troops from India had captured Java in August 1811.

Owing to scarce forage, one squadron of the 3rd Dragoons had moved to Idanha a Nova just before Christmas.

No. 8.   C[astelo] Branco,
                                          Jany 9th 1812.
My Dear Father,

I probably should not have written to you again so soon had I not been recently relieved from a state of perfect Insolvency by the arrival of four eight Dollar Pieces from Mr Sealy, being part of the Cash for a Draft of Stevenson and C^o. for £26. s13. d4

(100 dollars) and I now trust, like the Oxford Tradesmen, to be able to stand the Racket until the Payments are regularly made to the Reg^t.

Amongst the numerous Inconveniences attending this non-payment of Troops none is much greater than the wonderful Digestive Powers it causes both to Officers and Men. Amongst the former, myself and three others have in the course of the last Month absolutely eaten a silver Watch, four Folio Volumes, a Horse Hair Mattress and a Jack Ass—rather an extraordinary Bill of Fare for British Officers. Our Men have taken a great Fancy to the forage Corn belonging to the Horses, and in order to put a stop to such ravenous Appetites we have been under Necessity of flogging every Irishman and many twice or three Times over.

I believe in my last Letter I complained of the extreme cold Weather which I might well do, for the very Night that Letter was sent off, we were vizited by a very unusual fall of Snow which continued for 24 Hours and was then succeeded by a Deluge of Rain for two or three Days. The Weather is now become perfectly fine again and will, I trust, continue so as nothing can be more uncomfortable than a rainy Day in Portugal; in short the Misery is so great that words cannot express it without the Aid of a small Drawing which you here have in the section of a Portuguese street:—

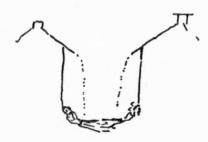

Of evils choose the least. If you walk close to the Wall, you certainly tread in a P - - - -, more in the centre [you] are deluged from the House Tops, and in the Middle [you] are in a Gutter up to your Knees in Water.

The only News from HeadQuarters is that Lord Wellington

removed them from Frenêda to Gallegos, another Village much nearer to Ciudad Rodrigo. I have likewise heard that Rations of Rum have lately been stopt from the Men in order, it is supposed, to have a sufficient Quantity for the Men working in the Trenches. From Gen. Hill we hear nothing.

We are daily in expectation of Marshal Beresford [who commands the Portuguese Army] with an alarming Retinue of Deputies, Assistants and Aides de camp, who will of course bolt us from our billets. The Marshal says he has reduced his Staff to the lowest, although still consisting of 63 Officers.

I shall always be obliged to you or Mr Egerton for any Hints you can give me as I have already profitted considerably by them. With regard to the Muslin Dress it sounds too much like a Luxury to be found in Portugal, indeed I have asked at some shops for it without success; in short cleanliness, comfort or neatness are words for which the Portuguese have no Term whatever.

I have received a Letter from Jack dated at Cambridge but as he is now at Sadborow I shall not answer his Letter until he returns to the University. His Manuscript Sermons will be excellent. We take three Weekly Papers and I believe Mr Bell's may be considered the best, infamous as it is. I sometimes get a Peep at a Ministerial Paper or should otherwise believe England was turned the wrong way upwards. One of these chaste Vehicles of Veracity observes on the taking of Batavia; 'The Invaders shew their Gallantry, the invaded submit, a new proof given of British valour and a new Burden laid on British Shoulders'— almost the whole notice taken of it.

All the Reports relating to Sir W. Pole's leaving Shute are equally creditable to that worthy Baronet. A correspondent from Plymouth informs me that the dread of a Horse whipping from an angry Farmer had occasioned his precipitate Retreat.

Do in your next Letter tell me what you think of the present State of Affairs; you cannot write to a more staunch Ministerial Man or one more sanguine in the present cause.

I am just setting off for Idanha a Nova where a Squadron is quartered, and think I deserve a Dinner for volunteering a Ride of twenty Miles over a Portuguese Road.

With Love to all at Home, believe me your dutiful Son,
WILLIAM BRAGGE.

Yours of the 25th Decr arrived at Cas[telo] Branco (150 miles from Lisbon) on the 5th Jan^{ry} 1812.

I am sorry to hear so indifferent an Account of Mr Egerton's Health and beg to be kindly remembered to him and his amiable Partner.

Notwithstanding the continuance of the very fine Weather. out sick Soldiers do not rally as might be expected—the Ague, Dissentry and Fevers are the prevailing Disorders. I do believe hanging is not more essentially necessary in St Giles's than in the Medical department of this Army. In the General Hospital at this Place, consisting of about 300 Soldiers, they frequently bury Twenty in a Week.

[On cover: LISBON JA 26 1812]

On 12 January, the Regiment was ordered up to the front to cover the siege of Ciudad Rodrigo. William's next letter was written on the day after the capture of the town.

No. 9.
Aldeia da Ponte,
Jan^{ry} 20th 1812.

My Dear Father,

After having given you so many rumours of events likely to take place in this Peninsula, you may suppose I have infinite satisfaction in informing you that one at least of my numerous Predictions is already accomplished by the Bombardment of Ciudad Rodrigo, in addition to which, I shall probably be enabled to confirm an account of its fall before this Letter is closed, as the Firing which we could distinctly hear and see during the whole of Yesterday has entirely ceased to Day; but of this I can give you better Intelligence when Major Clowes (who rode over Yesterday) returns.

The Village of Aldeia da Ponte, from whence this Letter is sent, is about 14 Miles from Ciudad Rodrigo, 1 Mile and a half from the frontier and 3 Miles from Sabugal and Alfaiates, so you perceive we have marched a good Trip to the North since I last wrote to you. The Village itself is truly wretched, but some heretic Soldiers having built a Chimney and Fire Place in the corner of almost every Room, it is during the present severe Frost by far the most agreeable Place after Sunset that we have seen in Portugal.

We started on the Twelfth with five days Forage for Man and Beast and arrived here on the fifth Day without having broken any of the Horses' Knees or Backs, and are now ready for Signor Marmont and his Cavalry as soon as he chooses to march this way. Indeed considering the Nags have only eight Pounds of Corn a day and no Forage but what the Dragoons pull up by the Roots, they are in surprising Condition.

During this March we have seldom been in Pallaces but very often in Pigstyes and I do not recollect ever having felt it colder of a Night in England; perhaps this may in some Measure be accounted for by the unusual Quantity of 'Heaven's own blessed Light' perceivable through the different Holes in the Roof of the Cottages, all of which have suffered more or less by the frequent Vizits of the French Army.

The Fifth Division of our Army passed through the Morning we arrived here, composed partly of English and partly of Portuguese. It is difficult to conceive a greater contrast than that existing between this Allied Army; the English, all in new Cloathes and good Appointments, well fed and looking if possible in better spirits than in England, were followed by the Portuguese in the raggedest of all possible ragged Cloathes, in addition to which they were much lower in Stature and appeared all to be thinking of the Approaching Danger. As Major Clowes may possibly give me a little News at his Return, I shall delay writing any more for a few hours.

Afternoon 20th Jan^ry 1812.

An Amateur having returned from the scene of Action, I can fully confirm the account of the Surrender of Ciudad Rodrigo, which was carried by Assault last Night between the Hours of 8 and 9 by 300 Volunteers from the Light Division and a Column of the 3rd Division. Two Breaches had been established in the Walls after 5 Days' Bombardment and from all accounts our Lads have never met with a warmer Reception.

The Governor and all the Garrison are Prisoners but as yet we Know nothing of the Numbers, probably between one or two Thousand.[27] On our part between two and Three hundred are killed and wounded, amongst the latter are Generals Craufurd, Vandaleur, and Col. Napier who lost an Arm.[28]

Nothing is known about our future Destination. Marmont will be at Salamanca this Day and can be with us by the 26th, but it is supposed he will scarcely venture a Battle.

With the exception of Gen¹ Hill's Division, who is now far advanced into Spain, the whole Allied Army are within 20 Miles of this Village. Our Cavalry ready for the Field are about 3,000.

Thank heavens we are to receive a Month's Pay tomorrow, the First money since we landed in the country.

It is impossible for so great an Army to remain in this Neighbourhood any length of Time, therefore we shall probably take another long march before I again write to you; and as long as the Weather continues dry and my Horses' Backs sound, I would as soon be employed in marching as in strolling about the dirty Streets of their Cities.

My Information is generally obtained in such curious Ways that you must not venture to quote my Authority or I shall get laughed at, for instance, I incidentally heard this Morning that Gen¹ Hill and his Division were again returned to Portalegre.[29]

Be kind enough to give my Love to my Mother and the whole Family Circle. Believe me Your dutiful Son, WILLIAM BRAGGE.

21st January 1812.
[On Cover: LISBON FE 08 1812 Received Feb⁣ʳʸ 20, answered 25.]

CHAPTER TWO

Cavalry Screen for Badajoz

January 1812–May 1812

Marmont heard of the fall of Ciudad Rodrigo on 21 January when he was eleven miles north east of Salamanca coming to the help of the fortress with some 12,000 men. The loss of the key frontier town was a severe blow and he had little wish to commit himself against Wellington's numerically superior concentration.

As soon as it was safe to do so, Wellington dispersed his troops to Winter Quarters again. The cavalry were the first to march away, since forage was scarce and a large supporting force no longer needed. The 3rd Dragoons left directly after the fall of the town, passed through Guarda and Seixo in the Mondego valley and halted near Arganil in the hills above the river.

William wrote again at the end of this march. Cartwright was a military outfitter. The map and telescope were elusive for over a year.

No. 10.   Falques,
                                                         Janry 24th 1812.

My Dear Father,

It is a literal Fact that I yesterday Morning wrote you a Letter complaining heavily of the Neglect and Idleness of all my Correspondents, but having in the course of the Day received one from you and another from Lucy making the same charge against me, I was induced to destroy my former Epistle with a Detirmination to blame the Winds and Waves in Future, who certainly are most execrable Post Masters. I must at the same Time justify myself by informing you that I wrote as soon as I had recovered my Nerves after the Retreat [from the Agueda to Sabugal in October] and again at Xmas.

As a Serjeant belonging to the Troop I command is shortly to come up from Belem, I have little doubt of receiving the

Telescope and Map, the latter of which will afford me many an Hours amusement in the next Campaign. Major Clowes is [temporarily] returned to England and his Box of Clothes arrived here for sale, but I can hear nothing of a Parcel which Cartwright was to send me enclosed in it. If it is in any of Cartwright's Boxes or should Clowes have taken it to Lisbon, I shall receive it, but all our Things have been so repeatedly opened to guard against the Wet that I fear it is lost.

I have seen the 29th *Bulletin* of the French Army which I really supposed a Fabrication at first. The loss of the Grand Army must have been immense and the Russians conducted with the greatest skill and bravery, but I wish they would be more candid in their own Account of Losses, as slaying Ten Thousands with the loss of a few Hundreds is too much like the Guerrilla Parties of Spain. The English are as superior to the French as the Russians, and they invariably meet a desperate resistance—and I must say that the Retreats of the French Army always excite a Sentiment of Astonishment and Respect in the British. The same newspaper gives us a Gazette Account of our losses, which I am delighted to find so trifling. I know that the Gazette is an exaggerated Account of Losses upon all these occasions but in our last Retreat I almost believed I had seen more than 300 wretched in the Road unable to move. All our Men and Horses have joined the Regiment, having been conducted (together with 150 Stragglers) almost through the French Army by the Brunswick Officer who was supposed to have *maintained* his Post above Burgos in order to be taken by the French. The contrary proves to have been the Fact as he escaped from Prison, collected these unfortunates, and with only two mounted Dragoons to do his outpost Duty, marched round the French and brought his Forces to Head Quarters. It is worthy of Observation that these Men received the greatest Assistance from the Spaniards and were never refused Rations until they got into Portugal.[1]

I sincerely hope the French Army in the North has received too great a shock to allow any great Reinforcements being sent to Spain. If that is the case, I should recommend Bounaparte to address his Brother [Joseph] and Marshals with 'Apostoli loquibantur' the next time Lord Wellington crosses the Agueda. I hope his Lordship's visit to Cadiz will be the means of putting the Spanish Armies on a better footing as in their present condition they are serious Injury to their Country and Cause.[2]

Scarcity of Forage induced them to move us from Seixo and the same reason must shortly occasion another March, when I trust we shall cross the Mondego and enter a level and fertile Country. Our Head Quarter is Arganil, and I am detached with a Newgate Crew to a Village about 3 Miles off absolutely buried amidst the Mountains of Estrêla, from the summit of which the Sea is clearly visible on a fine Day. Our situation is truly romantic and Picturesque—rather too much for me—as we are consequently drenched every third Day with Rain and have sight of the Sun for four Hours a Day only. Many Children three years old I should suppose had not gone far enough from their own Doors to see the Bright Orb of Day.

Curiosity prompted me to vizit Coimbra, the celebrated seat of Portuguese Learning, where 5 years ago the Greek Class amounted to only seven Scholars. At present there are not so many and I never recollect being so ill paid for so dreadful a Ride. The surrounding Country is more beautiful than any part of Portugal I had previously seen and the River at Coimbra Oxonians might Envy and certainly are more deserving of it than a set of Lubbers who content themselves with being Punted up and Down by way of Recreation. The Town and Students are equally dirty and the numerous Convents and Colleges built with no more Architectural Tastes than our Manufactories at Chard and elsewhere, and in every point of View the Town has more the appearance of a manufactory than a University. The Dress of the Students is becoming, but Gentlemen should wear Breeches.

There is some juggling going forward with regard to the Troops in our Reg[t] which I do not understand, but shall speak to Lord Charles [Manners, A.D.C. to Lord Wellington] about it to Day.[3] Our Army List now stands thus:—

> Lieuts. Shakespear
> Burn
> Bowater Adj.
> Bragge.

We have already one Troop unsold which Shakespear does not purchase because he is promised a Company. Burn promised to purchase it but then cried off on account of the extravagant Price asked for it, or—I rather imagine—because he knows his Brother-in-law will sell his as soon as ordered on Service. After Burn I am the next claimant, but not having served Three Years it would be useless making any application. Should an opportunity offer upon my completing my Apprenticeship, it would be of considerable Advantage to make the Purchase as the Captains leave to suit their own convenience and not yours, and have therefore not the slightest claim to any Sum beyond the Regulation, which I believe is seldom the case in England. Should you purchase me a Troop in the Summer, I shall be a Captain before many others have obtained their Lieutenantcies who entered the Army at the same Time, and thus be on a level with others of Seven Years standing—so great has been the Promotion.

At the End of this last Campaign I had scarcely a Rag left and no Boots. I have therefore purchased the whole of a deceased Officer's Clothes, which he had ordered from Cartwright. I do not know whether I am to pay the Taylor or the Officer's Executors but I shall at any rate be obliged to you to lodge me some more money in Greenwood's Hands as the New Mare has nearly drained that Store. I have at present 40£ in my Pocket and 4 Months' Pay due, with (I believe) 23£ in Stephenson's Bank, and one Horse for Sale, which will bring me 40 or 50£ whenever she is sold, therefore I hope it will be some Time before I again apply to you for Money.

We are all dreaming of Peace, but as only the Opposition Papers hint at such an event, I conclude it is not very probable, tho' I do not see that Napoleon has much to concede or we anything to ask, which he might not readily grant without Injury to his Empire, as Spain, under the existing circumstances, is scarcely of any Value to him. Having freed Spain and Portugal whilst Russia has relieved herself, I do not conceive but what it might be obtained, tho' we should have some Difficulty in binding him over to keep the Peace.

Lucy writes me word that her Husband has again broke his Head in a drunken fit. How angry the bold would be, if I was to tell him Gigs and Horses were his worst Enemies and that he had better walk on foot in Future.

We have just received another remount of very excellent

IV. Major-General John Gaspard Le Marchant.
From a miniature painted by P. Jean in 1787.

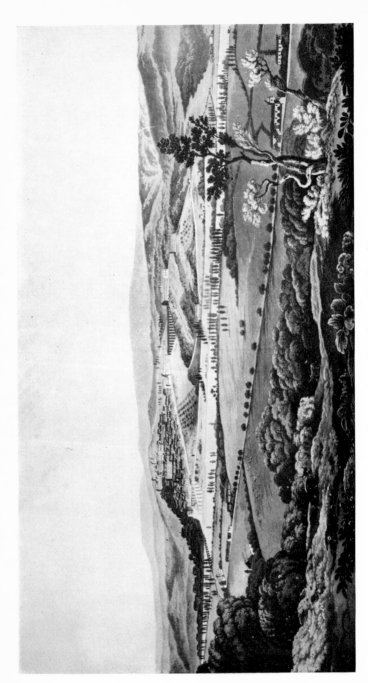

V. City of Coimbra from the South.

From an engraving of 1815.

Horses but as men and not Horses are wanted, they must go to pieces before the Spring. Our Troop has lost 55 Horses and 23 Men, besides Invalids gone to England. Others have lost the same number, therefore you might almost calculate the Average loss of British Horses at about 300 Horses per Annum each Reg^t.

With Love to my Mother and Sister, Believe me, Your dutiful Son, WILLIAM BRAGGE.

P.S. I have unfortunately lost my Seal with the Arms on it.

[On Cover: LISBON]

The lack of forage in the countryside which had been laid waste during Masséna's campaign in the previous winter compelled the Regiment to move again—this time to Fundão. William wrote from there in the first week in February.

Le Marchant's brigade now comprised the 5th Dragoon Guards and 3rd Dragoons, and the 4th Dragoons who replaced the 4th Dragoon Guards. The brigade remained unchanged for the rest of the War.

No. 11.   Fundão,
                                    Febry 4th 1812.

My Dear Father,

A Three day's March has again brought us out of a Tract of Country so completely desolated by the repeated Movements of contending Armies that a longer stay would certainly have starved half the Horses. We were sometimes without Corn, had never a larger Allowance than 6 lbs a Day, and could procure no species of long Forage but such as the Men pulled up by the Roots, I have, however, one Satisfaction in proving that my own Horses can stand upon short Rations as well as their Neighbours and have returned here, thin enough, but all well and without any Sore Backs.

Fundão, where we are now likely to remain some Time, is the best Town we have seen and has suffer'd but little from the French who remained only Five Days in the Neighbourhood [in March 1811].The Town is situated in the Valley of the Zezere, a valley formed by that River running between the Alpedrinha Mountains and the Serra da Estrêla, the highest Land in

D

Portugal. It is very Fertile and beautifully Picturesque, not to mention the Alpedrinha Wine which is extremely good and only a Shilling a Quart.

I shall always regret having lost two sights by this short allowance of Forage, one was Ciudad immediately after the Siege, and the other a Fox chase with Ld Wellington's Hounds, where he and Old Graham (the second-in-command of the British Army) were both riding for the Brush.[4] His Lordship's Hounds are in excellent condition and very Handsome. I mentioned some Time ago that we intended establishing a Pack of Harriers next Season, which our Friends at Canterbury [the cavalry depôt] are already completing very fast.

The variety of Lodgings I get into on a March is really amusing; at Sabugal My Bed was composed of a Pillow, a Rug, *two dirty Petticoats* and two large Towels, and all this in a House where they take Portuguese Lodgers. I got some Lice of course, and the next night had a Superb Suit of Apartments at Caria with a Bed in the Patron's Library. I should not have been so miserably off at Sabugal but my old Horse who was honoured with the Baggage took an opportunity of lying down in the River, much to the annoyance of my Bed and Blankets.

I see by the London Papers that the Rainy Season in Portugal commenced some Months since, although I never saw any Quantity of wet Weather until within these few Days but from the Situation of this Place I should imagine it rained three Days for one in any other Part of Portugal.

Every Body supposes that Ld Wellington, having driven the French out of Portugal, repaired the Fortifications of Almeida, garrisoned and considerably strengthened the Town of Ciudad Rodrigo, will now turn his Attention to Badajoz, the second important pass into the Kingdom; but as I know he has talked about it in every Company, I cannot help thinking that he has not the most distant Idea of going near the Place.

We are all much pleased with a recent change in the Brigade, by which we lose the Fourth or Royal Irish Dragoon G^ds and get the Fourth or Queen's own Dragoons, the Reg^t with which we were Brigaded for 3 Years at Canterbury.[5]

I am sorry to hear you have suffer'd so much from Rheumatism which I trust will have left you long before you receive this Letter.

Be kind enough to give my Love to all at Home and Believe me Your dutiful Son, WILLIAM BRAGGE.

P.S.

Ld Euston is now with us and is a very agreeable young Man with very little of the Lord about him.

I was very glad to hear that Sir William Oglander had bought the Chestnut Horse, which certainly ought to stand farthest from the Stable Door, unless the Baronet has made considerable alterations in his Stud since last Season.

[On Cover: LISBON FE 29 1812]

The dreadful weather conditions on the Portuguese border at the beginning of February finally decided Marmont to return to Valladolid. Wellington had anticipated this but he was now free to complete plans for the seizure of Badajoz—irrespective of William's private reservations.

With the exception of the 5th Division and Victor Alten's cavalry brigade, all the Army marched south, beginning on 19 February. The 3rd Dragoons left Fundão on the 26th.

William's next letter was written in mid-March as Wellington was closing in on Badajoz.

Sir David Dundas, generally known as 'Old Pivot', was C.-in-C. of the Army during the period the Duke of York was out of favour.

No. 12.   Borba,
                                                 14th March 1812.
My dear Father,

I have this instant received your Letters of the 5th and 26th February together with one from Charlotte and another from Cox, all brought by the same Mail and as we are again likely to move within the next Four and twenty Hours, I shall lose no Time in answering them.

With regard to any future Movements or probable Events, no one can be more in the dark than myself for although in the very center of the British Army, surrounded with Generals and only 4 Leagues from Elvas (the present HeadQuarters), I cannot find any one hardy enough to venture a Conjecture of what is likely to take Place, therefore for the present I must content myself with giving a brief account of our late Movements.

We left Fundão on the 28th [corrected to 26th later], passed through Castelo Branco and recrossed the River Tagus at Vila Velha, where we passed over about five Months since, and halted one Day at Niza, from which Place to Borba the Country was entirely new to us and indeed so different from what we had hitherto seen of Portugal that I could scarcely believe so great a contrast could possibly exist in the same Kingdom. The Country itself is quite open, tolerably level, and the greater part of it in the highest State of Cultivation. The Roads [are] equal to any in the New Forest and the Towns and Villages more delightfully *clean* and neat than any thing we see in England, every House and Cottage nicely Whitewashed within and without, all the Churches and Public Buildings standing detached, the Streets very wide and not a Bit of Filth to be seen, whilst the Pots and Pans, highly polished and arranged in order over a good Fire Place, render every Cottage in the Alentejo a more desirable Residence than the most sumptuous Houses North of the Tagus. Estremoz is the only Town of considerable Note we had to pass through and I assure you it is a most beautiful place, although surrounded with a Nest of Massive Walls and ditches. I saw there 16 Twenty Four Pounders on their Road to Badajoz, which together with as many more of the same Calibre form only a Part of the immense Train destined for the Reduction of that Place.[6]

We are terribly crowded here with Infantry. Four Regts march away this Morning and as many again succeed them this Afternoon but I am inclined to think we shall ourselves march Tomorrow.

Genl Le Marchant has his whole Brigade within reach of him and has therefore begun playing Soldiers in order to prove the efficiency of some miserable awkward Manoeuvres which he has himself been coining. I have no doubt they all occurred to Sir David [Dundas] but were rejected for others infinitely superior. Be that as it may, our Schoolmaster had the three Regts out yesterday and would I have no doubt treat us with more Field Days should opportunities offer themselves.

I sincerely wish the French could see the 5th Dragoon Guards in their present condition. They have scarcely a Horse under 15 Hds 2 Ins and their Men are nearly as tall as the Life Guards, the whole in as good order as when they left England and as they have never Trimmed or cut their Horses' Tails since that Time, every Horse has the exact appearance of a West Country Stallion. The Reg^t at present has a most Formidable Look but a little Starvation and Work will I fear soon reduce them.

We are only two Miles from Vila Viçosa, a Town famed in Story for having been the Residence of the Braganza Family, the Pallace, Tombs, Park and Armoury of which are the great Lions of the Country. The Park is eighteen Miles in Circumference and very little worth seeing but contains a large Herd of Deer, some Boars and beautiful Red Deer.[7] As for the Armoury, it is so far in a state of Decay that the Farriers of the Green Horse [the 5th D.G.] are (Technically speaking) working it up— a real Fact—a young Tounsend of the 14th [is] shooting the Deer in the Park.

One Matthews, a ci-devant Servant of Capt Adney's, marched out this Morning with the 51st. I have watched him narrowly and can safely say he has not been sober since we came to the Town.

You cannot conceive anything more grateful to the Taste of a Thirsty Man than the Borba Wine, which is certainly the finest in Portugal and agrees better with the English Constitution than any other Liquor.

I am just going to receive another Month's Pay and the Bat and Forage money up to the 24th of Jan^ry, therefore we cannot any longer complain of our arrears: the whole Army being paid up to that period.

March 17th 1812.
Olivenza–Spain.

I delayed sending this Letter from Borba in consequence of having received one from Mr Sealy of Lisbon informing me that my Draft for *100 Dollars,* drawn on Stephenson and Co, had been protested by them, an event I am somewhat vexed at as it has so much the Appearance of Swindling. I shall immediately send Mr Sealy his Money but shall probably be obliged to give a Draft on you to a Brother Officer who wishes to lodge a small Sum in England. There are two Stephensons Bankers in London which might have occasioned this mistake, although I specified late Batson & Co.

We are pushed on here in a hurry with two Troops of Horse Artillery and two Cavalry Regiments. 3 Divisions crossed the Guadiana this Day to invest Badajoz, the Ground before which will be broken immediately. In short every thing has in this Neighbourhood such a Warlike Aspect that I intend putting a Stone in my Pistol and making three Ball Cartridges Tomorrow.

Give my Love to my Mother and all the Family and Believe me Your dutiful Son, WILLIAM BRAGGE.

P.S.

This Place is 3 Leagues from Badajoz and I believe 12 from any French Force except that Garrison.

While active preparations for the assault of Badajoz were being made, a covering force of three divisions and two cavalry brigades (Slade's and Le Marchant's) moved southwards to keep Soult's possible reinforcements from Seville at a respectable distance from the beseigers.

William wrote to his father from Fuente del Maestre at the beginning of April, mentioning the odd scuffle in the early hours of 26 March and the Regiment's sharp encounter on the First of the month.

No. 13.   Fuente del Maestre,
                               3 Leagues from Villafranca.
                                       April 5th 1812.

My dear Father,

We have for this Month past continued in such alarm and Confusion that I very much doubt whether my last Letter (dated at Olivenza) was ever sent from the Brigade Major's Office and as there is a great Probability of such an Event having taken place, I shall give you as nearly as I can recollect a Journal of our late Proceedings commencing with our March from Fundão, which took place on the 26th of Febry. On the 5th March we arrived at Borba, having in our Route passed through Castelo Branco, recrossed the Tagus at Vila Velha and halted one one Day at Niza. From thence to Borba the Country was entirely new to us, indeed it was almost another World so great a contrast exists between the Two Sides of the Tagus, Nothing can possibly exceed the Misery and Filth of the North, whereas in the Alentejo every House, Town and Village are equally remarkable for their extreme beauty, cleanliness and regularity of Building; the Streets are all nearly as Broad as the widest in Lisbon and publick Buildings of every description detached from the Crowd of Houses.

We left Borba on the 14th and on the 16th forded the Guadiana at Juromenha and arrived the same Night at Olivenza, the Frontier Town of Spain on this Quarter. From thence we pushed on rapidly as far as Zafra and Medina de las Torres, driving small Parties of the Enemy before us every Day and receiving the kindest Treatment from the Spaniards fairly worn to death by the constant Requisitions of the French, who support their Troops entirely in this arbitrary manner. On the 25th we were moved sine Baggage to Bienvenida, where we joined General Graham who had with him 10,000 Infantry and Genl Slade's Brigade of Cavalry. The same Evening we advanced with this Force to Llerena, intending to surprise the Enemy who had about 1,000 Infantry and 200 Cavalry quartered in that Town.[8] This Expedition beggars all description; we marched on without any advance guard except Sir T. Graham, Sir S. Cotton and numerous Staff who were met about 3 in the Morning by a small Patrole of the Enemy who immediately fired and Galloped back. This circumstance alarmed our noble Leaders who faced about and at Speed dashed in amongst the Infantry. The Night was dark and the Brunswick Oels Infantry in front, who, supposing themselves attacked by the French Cavalry, sans Ceremonie wheeled into Line and fired a Volley, seconded by the 51st, but having fortunately faced the wrong way the whole of their Balls flew across the column of Cavalry and another Column of Infantry marching on a Parallel direction. This Circumstance put all the Cavalry to Flight and for about half an Hour created the greatest Confusion, not to mention the Alarm given to the Enemy, the Death of two Officers and some Privates who thus fell Victims to the unsteadiness of our Noble Staff. We arrived at Llerena at Day Break but not before the Enemy had retired in the greatest Order [to Azuaga, eighteen miles farther East].[9] After this very Fatiguing Day, we again proceeded Southward as far as Azuaga, having again made an unsuccessful Attempt to surprise the Foe who with his usual alacrity retired as soon as a superior Force appeared in View. We remained some days at Azuaga (which you will find on S. Eastern

Extremity of Estremadura), keeping our Horses constantly
Baggaged and ready to turn out immediately, being on all sides
surrounded by the Enemy.[10] On the 2nd April [we] commenced
our Retrograde March and arrived yesterday at this Place,
having been relieved from this most harrassing Duty by Genl
Anson's Brigade, who can only advance one Stage beyond us
since Soult reached Llerena on 4th April. For six Days our
Horses have been constantly saddled and during the whole Time
have not received a Mouthful of Corn. I have two Sore backs
which will I hope be well again in a few Days. The little
Mare carries me surprizingly and has twice been honoured with
my Company for nearly 24 Hours.

I have already had two narrow Escapes, once from being shot
by the Oels and a day or two afterwards by being sent through
a Woody country to reconnoitre the Enemy whose Cavalry had
at the same Time crossed my Path with the Intention of surprising one of our Picquets, in which they nearly succeeded by
the extreme unsteadiness of young Troops. As it was we only
lost 10 Men and Horses.[11]

Long before you receive this Letter Badajoz must have fallen,
as there are at this Moment Three practicable Breaches and 38
Twenty Four Pounders within 200 Y^ds of the Wall besides 25
Bombs constantly throwing Shells at their Defences; nothing
was ever before undertaken on such a magnificent Scale. Soult
is certainly advancing but as their whole Force in and near
Estremadura does not exceed 28,000 Men, there is no chance of
his gaining any thing but a Beating if he attempts an Engagement, which would take Place at Albuera again if any thing
was attempted.[12]

If you received my last Letter you are Informed that for some
unknown reason Mr Stephenson protested my draft for 100
Dollars payable to Mr Sealy, who of course considers me a
Humbug. Should we ever again get into settled Quarters, I shall
remit him his Money in Cash and draw upon you for 50£.

I received yours of the 10th of March whilst on a Picquet
about 3 Miles from Azuaga and was extremely sorry to hear so
poor an account of my Mother's Health whose Attention to her
amiable Neighbours at Thorncombe has already occasioned
about three serious Indispositions. I heartily wish your next
Letter may give a better Acc^t of her.

I have lately added a good Mule to my Establishment which was rendered absolutely necessary by the extraordinary way in which General Officers work subalterns and their Nags. If poor Adney was so much employed he would have greater Reason for his constant Prayers for Gen. Officers. Besides Picquets, Patroles and other light Duties, every Genl chooses to have an Intelligent Subaltern to ride with him as Aid de Camp, who is of course obliged to keep his pace.

I sincerely hope we may shortly have a general Engagement, the result of which would beyond doubt be glorious to the British Army, give Confidence to the Spaniards, expel the French from Estremadura and consequently raise the Siege of Cadiz. At present the Spaniards know not whom to trust; they detest the French but at the same Time dread their Power and from having seen us so repeatedly advance and retire, cannot give us credit for the Force which we certainly posses. Now could we take Badajoz and beat the French decidedly in one great Battle, neither Estremadura, the neighbourhood of Cadiz or indeed any part of Andalusia would be longer tenable.

With love to all the Family and my earnest Prayers for my Mother's speedy recovery, I remain in great haste Your dutiful Son, WILLIAM BRAGGE.

P.S.

I am perhaps scarcely justified in telling you I have no opinion of our General's Abilities and very little confidence in the K.O.D., a Troop of whom have lost a noble opportunity—Time must show.

For the next month the 3rd Dragoons were almost constantly in the saddle. The screening cavalry and infantry in advance of Badajoz retired to a defensive position at Albuera as Soult's relief force drew closer. The French Marshal could do no more though, and when he learnt that the fortress had fallen on the night of 6 April, he had no wish to expose his weaker force longer than necessary. He fell back on Llerena, observing that he 'could not fight the whole English Army'.[13] Le Marchant's brigade followed him south and a lively cavalry action took place near the small town on the 11th.

The same day Le Marchant's brigade and other units were recalled to Portugal to dislodge Marmont. Reluctantly obeying

Napoleon's unrealistic orders, the Commander of the Army of Portugal had set out from Salamanca at the end of March with 20,000 men and fifteen days' supplies to thrust half-heartedly into the province of Beira. When he reached the Agueda, Victor Alten (commanding the only cavalry brigade north of the Tagus) took alarm, fell back on Castelo Branco and even crossed the river—contrary to Wellington's orders. But for the steadiness and firm action of Brig. Gen. Lecor, the Governor of the Province, an embarrassing situation could have arisen.

The 3rd Dragoons marched north through Badajoz in mid-April, reaching Castelo Branco on the 23rd. Marmont had, however, begun to withdraw more than a week before, due, he wrote, 'to being starved out of Portugal rather than to any offensive allied action'.[14]

The Regiment remained north of the Tagus for five days longer then returned to the Alentejo and dispersed to cantonments around Cabeço de Vide during the first week in May.

William wrote to his brother-in-law once during these marches and to his father when he was again in settled quarters. Some details in earlier letters are repeated and he recapitulates in a long list his movements since the end of February.

Gum Cistus, mentioned in the letter of 6 May, is a mountain rock rose about two feet high. Even today 'where arable land gives place to an outcrop of barren rocky hill . . . [it] . . . covers the harsh soil with an airy cloud of immense white blossoms like butterflies arrested in flight'.[15]

No. 14.

Addressed to: Capt. ADNEY,
SOUTH DEVON REGt NOTTINGHAM
ENGLAND

> Alpalhão,
> a dirty village one League
> distant from Niza.
> April 21st 1812.

Amidst the Toils and Troubles of War, I feel inclined to spare some few Moments in order to acknowledge the Receipt of two Letters from my dear Brother and Sister, both of which arrived within 3 Days of each other, although dispatched from England by different Packets, and I was happy to find the superscription of each ornamented with Numbers as if promising a more regular Correspondence.

Lucy's Letter I received amongst the Ruins of Badajoz, where we recrossed the Guadiana on 16th April after having twice traversed the whole Province of Spanish Estremadura without in any Degree forwarding the Views of the Spanish Patriots, who are—I have no doubt—very fine Fellows but I never have yet had the Pleasure of seeing any one Individual in Arms during the whole Month we remained in the Country.

Never were Troops so harrassed with Marching as we have been since the first of Jany, having in that Time gone nearly 800 Miles and have now no prospect of a Halt although our Horses are worn to Skeletions and our Backsides to Thread Paper—but it is no use grumbling especially as the Weather continues Fine.

We passed down the Alentejo (which is by far the most beautiful Country I ever saw) by way of Niza, Crato, Estremoz and Borba, crossed the Guadiana between Juromenha and Olivenza continuing our Route by Sta. Marta, Los Santos, Zafra, Llerena and so to Azuaga, which is quite on the Frontier of Andalusia [and] where we remained constantly Saddled for about a Week. We in turn retreated by the same Road to the Fatal Plains of Albuera, where we encamped for one Night expecting a fight in the morning, but the French having again retired we proceeded by forced Marches as far as Llerena. [There] Sir S. Cotton with the assistance of all the British Cavalry contrived to take about 150 French, losing 24 Horses, 12 Men [killed] and 38 wounded,[16] not to mention his having thrown the whole concern four Days in rear of the Infantry, who are marching to the North to encounter Mr Marmont, who, during Ld Wellington's absence, had advanced as far into Portugal as Castelo Branco, leaving Ciudad Rodrigo closely invested and very short of Provisions. Our present Route is for Castelo Branco where we shall arrive the day after tomorrow and Report says the French are to oppose us about six Leagues to the North of it, so Here ends an acct of our late Adventures.

I sincerely wish we may be able to penetrate into Spain as the People are in every Respect superior to the Portuguese but in no one particular more so than in the Beauty of the Signoras, who are, generally speaking, very pretty and decently clean.

On my Return to Fuente del Maestre, I found my old Quarters occupied by an Officer of the Ninth, who was under the necessity of shifting, but not before he had asked me to dinner, being—I suppose—struck with the Elegance of my Attire and Manners. I refused his Invitation and cast a Sheep's Eye at his Baggage where Lt Ker, 9th Dragoons, was very conspicious on about 50 Boxes. This meeting was whimsical enough and will probably occasion a Laugh if ever I have the Pleasure of seeing his Lady. He is a pretty Man, remarkably neat and wears a Blue Velvet Forageing Cap, gold Tassel and Band of the same edged with white Ermine. How nice.

We subscribed a Dollar each and gave a Ball the same Night at Fuente del Maestre, which was well attended and of course particularly entertaining where neither Party understood the other's Language or mode of Dancing. The Fashionable dress is Black with a white Handkerchief and the Hair, which is particularly long, done up in a sort of Knot and skrewed into the Pole.

We passed through Badajoz about six days after its being taken and I assure you the sight was, still, shocking enough for me. The places where our Men escaladed the Walls, with every Weapon which the fertile Mind of a Frenchman could oppose to them, were full as high as the Top of our Breakfast Room Windows at Sadborow.[17] I don't know what John Bull will say to it but our loss has been tremendous, especially in Officers, 79 of whom were either killed or wounded in 3 Reg^{ts}.[18]

I have been nearly as much vexed about a tame Partridge as you. The Story is this: I caught the Bird close to Borba and thinking to place it in an Asylum for Life, gave it to a Beautiful Nun who kissed it a Thousand Times and produced it *dead* at the Grate in about 5 Minutes—

I at one Time had two sore backs out of 3 Horses but have contrived to get them well without a day's rest. Write soon and believe me to be with best wishes your Affectionate Brother,

WILLIAM BRAGGE.

[P.S.] I shall not be able to write to my Father for some Time, therefore let him know I am well and again in the North.

No. 15.   Vaiamonte,
                                                    May 4th 1812.

As this Sheet of Paper is extremely large and Anecdotes for a Letter proportionately scarce, I shall devote one half of it to a Journal of my late Adventures, which although by no means entertaining, will at any rate convince you that Ld Wellington can find as much Employment for heavy Dragoons as Light. I shall give you the Distances and Names of the Villages where we halted, most of which can be found in any Map of Spain and Portugal:

Feb^{ry}		Leagues
24th	Fundão	
25	Alcains	4
26	Castelo Branco	2
27	Sarnadas and other ruins	3
28	Niza	4

Crossed the Tagus at Vila Velha. Halted in consequence of a Blunder amongst our most excellent Staff, who by this means contrived to jam up 2 Reg^{ts} and 2 Troops of Horse Artillery in a Town scarcely affording covering for one Reg^t.

March		
2nd	Crato	4
3	Fronteira	4
5	Borba	2

Here we remained about Ten Days; ocassionally recreated with Field Days for amusement of the General.

15	Alandroal	2
16	Olivenza	

Crossed the Guadiana at Juromenha.

17	Nogales	4

Went with Sir S. Cotton to Sta. Marta. Saw a Frenchman.

18	Villa Alva	4
19	Los Santos	
21	Medina de las Torres	2

Passed through Zafra, which on account of its good shops is styled Little Seville.

25	Bienvenida	3

Arrived late in the Evening. Marched again at 10 O'Clock. Arrived at Llerena by Day Break with about 10,000 Infantry and two Heavy Brigades of cavalry. Shot at in the Night by our own People—all thrown in Confusion and the Enemy warned of our approach. Horse Artillery ordered to fire at a Dead Wall mistaken for Infantry. Did not get into Quarters until 5 of the Day 26th.

26	Villa Garcia	7
27	Valencia	3
28	Berlanga on Picquet	
29	Azuaga	2

Another Night Expedition with as Little success.

30	Azuaga	
31	La Granja on Picquet	

[April] . . . the French made a most furious Attack the next Evening and nearly succeeded in capturing 2 Squadrons.
1st The Men were panic Struck at their numbers and behaved dastardly.

I was sent on a reconnoitring Expedition to Fuenteovejuna—8 Leagues—and marched at 12 the same Night with the Brigade to

2	Valencia	6
3	Bienvenida	4
4	Los Santos	4
5	Fuente del Maestre	2

Trumpets ordered to sound 'To Horse' at Midnight because the Inhabitants should not be alarmed.

7	Almendral	6
8	Albuera	2

Passed the Day on the Fatal Plain of Albuera, still white with the Skeletons of last Year's Battle, and encamped with 4 Divisions of Infantry in the wood occupied by the French last Year.

Had not the French heard of the surrender of Badajoz, Albuera would again have been the scene of Action.

9	a Village	2
10	Los Santos	4

We arrived, in consequence of the usual Mistakes of the Staff, late in the Evening. Moved on at 12.

11 Bienvenida

Got to Bienvenida at Day break and 2 Leagues farther on came up with Anson's Brigade manouevring with 6 Squadrons of the Enemy. We continued trotting until the 5th Dragoon Gds (on our right) had an opportunity of charging, which they did most Gallantly. They routed the Enemy and raced them to Llerena, where some Cannon Shot and the Sight of 15,000 Men brought them up.

The Big Wigs choose to consider this Affair a great Feather in Sir Stapleton's Cap but when the superiority in Numbers and Horses is so much in our Favour together with the Ground, we ought not to think much of taking 4 Officers, 140 Men and 114 of the worst Horses you ever beheld. The Loss of the 5th Dragoon Guards was 12 killed, 2 missing, 1 Officer and 35 Men wounded, and 24 Horses missing. It is worthy of remark that scarcely one Frenchman died of his wounds, although dreadfully chopped, whereas 12 English Dragoons were killed on the Spot and others dangerously wounded by *thrusts*. If our men had used their Swords so, three Times the Number of French would have been killed. We had six Regts in the Field.[16]

12	Los Santos	4	
13	Fuente del Maestre	2	
14	Nogales	5	Wet
15	Val Verde	4	Wet
16	Badajoz	3	
17	Elvas	3	Wet
18	Estremoz	6	Wetter still
			Horses dying at a rate of 3 daily.
19	Fronteira	4	
20	Crato	4	
21	Alpalhão	2	
22	Vila Velha	6	Camp
23	Castelo Branco	4	
24	Alcains	2	
25	a Village	2	

I and two others slept in a Room six Feet by four, the Commissary in the Church, and Heywood turned a dead Woman out of her Quarters to make room for his Bed.

26	Povão	2	Luckily tacked in a heavy storm.
28	Sarnadas	5	Tacked about
29	Niza	5	Wet
30	Alpalhão	2	

May

| 1st | Flor de Rosa | 2 | Wet |
| 2 | Cabeço de Vide | 3 | |

I am detached to this Village with the right Squadron to refit.

Thus ended a Route of upwards of 180 Leagues and you will be surprised to hear that most of the Officers' Horses and many Troopers' are in better Condition now than when they started. We have sore Backs innumerable, chiefly oweing to the misjudged economy of the Home Establishment who are always afraid of commanding Officers being ruined by too great an expense in Saddles and other Appointments. My own Horses are in beautiful condition and both the Mare's Backs perfectly cured without a day's rest.

Vaiamonte,
May 6th 1812.

My Dear Father,

I have sent you as correct a Journal of our late marches and countermarches as I can now recollect and I think you will agree with me that Le Marchant's Brigade have done their Part towards walking the Enemy out of the Country. I was confoundedly vexed at Bienvenida when an order came for us to march to Castelo Branco with the delightful prospect of remaining all the summer amongst Gum Cistus and miserable Villages rendered Ten Thousand Times worse by the late Incursion of Marmont's Army. We got the other side of Castelo Branco and after wandering about for Three Days, received a Route for the South, where Report says we are to remain 3 Weeks undisturbed. The Villages we are quartered in are on the Road from Portalegre to Estremoz, 4 Leagues from each, in a delightful Country much like Hampshire and abounding with Corn, Cattle, Vegetables, Poultry and Game. Although so few Months from England, I already forget the state of Vegetation at this Season of the Year. In this Country the Rye is almost ripe, the Barley and Oats in ear and Beans fit to eat, the Lemons are not gathered and the Trees in full Blossom with their Fruit still hanging in clusters. If these People had one half the Taste for Gardens and Parks which the English have, every Quinta would be a perfect Paradise as they abound with Beautiful Water and have the most delightful Trees in the World, with Heaths, Myrtles and Flowers in abundance.

In consequence of the heavy Rains, we were forced to go round by way of Badajoz in order to cross the Guadiana, which gave us a fine opportunity of seeing that Place before the Breaches etc., were repaired. The Approaches and Batteries were quite levelled and most of the Bodies buried, but the Town itself and Walls exactly in the State in which it was when our Troops entered, of which you have already received better Accts than I

VI. Badajoz, as approached from Elvas.

From an aquatint in the collection of Col. Crookshank.

VII. Sadborow, two views.

can possibly write you, but depend on it no Newspaper can possibly give an exaggerated Account of the Difficulties and Dangers our men had to encounter. I understand that one Portuguese Brigade were so Panic struck at the Slaughter that they laid down to a Man but upon seeing the British still advancing, jumped up, and fought like Devils. One Fort was taken by the Portuguese alone, who rammed every Frenchman and brought the Officers off in puris Naturalibus. The Survivors richly deserved the Liberty of plundering the Town, an Indulgence they by no means abused, having left neither Money, Plate, Linen, Bottoms of Chairs nor any one Article of Furniture there was a possibility of carrying off. The Walls where Picton's Division escaladed is full as high as the Top of our Breakfast room Windows.[17]

I received yours of the 30th March at Castelo Branco in our Road up, and was much rejoiced to hear my Mother was recovering from her late Illness, which until then I had no Idea was of so serious a Nature. About that Time continual Riding, change of Weather or want of Vegetables brought on so many unpleasant Symptoms, that I had almost made up my mind to a Fever or Ague Fit, but upon applying to our pompous Aesculapius, I was informed the Golden Duct was stopped, Liver sluggish, Internals out of order etc. However a few Calomel Pills hurried all the Evil Genii through the Golden Duct with tremendous Explosions, leaving me in as good Health as ever.

The Good Sense, Conduct and Feeling of my two Brothers appear to go hand in hand and I firmly believe nothing but a good Flogging or a small command at such a Siege as Badajoz will ever open their Eyes to the many comforts they are likely to loose by such unprecedented Behaviour. I wish I had the Flogging of them with my Cat of eight Leathern Thongs taken out of a French Trumpeter's Kit at Llerena. It is a worse Instrument than ours and will be sent to Mr Whitbread if I have the good Fortune to bring it to England.

Whilst Lord Wellington was engaged at Badajoz, the French pushed into Portugal and were near destroying our Pontoon Bridge at Vila Velha. They plundered Castelo Branco, Covilhão and Fundão and must have made considerable Booty as all those Towns are inhabited by Bastard Jews, and had suffer'd but little by any former Incursion.

E

Being as much in Lord Wellington's Secret as any General Officer, I have as good a right to talk about what is to be done. He is himself in the Neighbourhood of Ciudad Rodrigo with (I believe) two Divisions of Infantry, 1st [German] Hussars, 11th Dragoons and heavy Germans. Genl Hill [is] in front of Badajoz with about 14,000 Men and 6 Regts of Cavalry, and all the rest of the Army in different Cantonments in the Alentejo,[19] therefore the Probability is that as soon as his Lordship can secure the North of Portugal, he will return here, collect his forces, join Genl Hill and advance in the Direction of Cordoba, where Soult's Army retired after the Surrender of Badajoz.[20]

It is supposed that Genl Baron Alten retired rather too rapidly from the North with the first [German] Hussars, which will, no doubt, draw down a handsome Panegyric on the German Generals from Messrs Burdett, Cobbett and Company.

I wrote to you twice when in Spain, but our Letters have to go through so many notable Hands that I much doubt whether you ever have or will receive them. I have paid Mr Sealy his hundred Dollars and shall shortly have to draw on you for 50£ in favour of a Quarter Master of our Regt. The Remount are at Lisbon, therefore the Parcel you sent Mr Cartwright will probably arrive very soon.

We have now charming Spring Weather tempting you out one hour, to make you wet to the Skin the Next—this has been the way for this last Fortnight, which will most likely be succeeded by a continuation of sultry dry weather for the next four Months.

Be kind enough to give my Love to my Mother and Charlotte, Believing me Your dutiful Son, WILLIAM BRAGGE.

May 6th 1812.

I have borrowed my Patron's Inkstand who performs the two important Offices of Parish Barber and Justice of the Peace.

[On Cover: LISBON MY 12 1812]

A fortnight later, William wrote again as the Regiment was about to march for Badajoz, having been called out in a hurry.

Hill, with a force of 7,000, raided Almaraz on 19 May.

No. 16.

Vaiamonte,
May 20th 1812.

My dear Father,

A Route has this moment arrived ordering us to march for Badajoz, and as there is no knowing where we may stop when once set in motion, I take the present opportunity of writing to you. The cause of this sudden order is, I believe, a movement of Drouet's on Merida, which is supposed to have alarmed Black Jack [Maj. Gen. Slade] who is in that quarter with his Brigade.[21]

By the same Post I have sent Mr Bean, Qr Master of the Third Dragoons, a Draft for Fifty Pounds drawn on Stevenson and Co. and payable at fourteen Days sight, and as he once protested a Draft I gave Mr Sealy, I should be obliged to you to prevent his repeating it, which would effectually spoil my Credit.

We have received Newspapers up to 28th of April, but I did not get any Letters by that Post. If we may trust the Accounts given in the Newspapers everything is going on as bad as possible in England.

I have written Lucy a long Letter and would have done the same to you had this Day been at my own disposal but as that is not the Case, you must give my Love to my Mother, Charlotte and the rest of the Family, believing me Your dutiful Son,

WILLIAM BRAGGE.

Ld Wellington is still in the North.
Genl Graham was two Days ago at Portalegre alone but will of course advance to his division. Hill has just destroyed the Bridge of Almaraz above Alcantara.

[On Cover: LISBON JU 3 1812. Answered June 8—No. 17]

CHAPTER THREE

Salamanca and Burgos: Triumph and Retreat

June 1812–December 1812

The capture of Ciudad Rodrigo and Badajoz opened the two high-roads into Spain. By the end of May Wellington had also achieved his two other objectives which were necessary safeguards for his summer campaign: the suspension bridge at Alcantara—a unique feat of military engineering—was completed whilst the bridge at Almaraz was denied to the French. His own internal north-south lines of communication were thereby markedly improved, whereas those between the two French armies, whose nearest link became Toledo, were seriously handicapped. He was now free to move against Soult or Marmont as he wished.

Leaving Hill with his corps of 18,000 (the 2nd Division, some Portuguese infantry and three brigades of cavalry) in the Estremadura, Wellington gathered up the rest of the Allied army of some 43,000 British, Germans and Portuguese in early June and marched towards the Army of Portugal.

At the end of the month William wrote from a village just north of Salamanca describing his part in the advance into Spain.

Marmont had assembled 5 of his 8 divisions—about 25,000 men—and advanced to face Wellington's strong defensive position on the heights of San Christobal, close to the north of Salamanca, on 19 June. Later he attempted to relieve the forts in the town by pushing along the south bank of the Tormes from Huerta. Le Marchant's brigade and two infantry divisions went to support Gen. Bock to repulse the French. The forts fell on 27th.

No. 17.   Village of Villares,
                                    3 miles from Salamanca.
                                    June 28th 1812.

My dear Father,

The Idea of having a tedious Business in the South of Spain, without any opportunity of writing or sending Letters to England induced me to send a short and hasty Epistle from Vaiamonte on the 20th of May, which I afterwards regretted, as we again returned to our old Quarters on the 27th without having performed any Thing of consequence except re-establishing all our sore Backs, which were before in a fair way towards recovery.

The cause of this little excursion of about 100 Miles has never been fully explained to us, but I firmly believe it was occasioned by General Slade's *retiring* from a Patrole of about 50 Men and immediately reporting that the Enemy were advancing towards Merida in considerable Force,[1] and as the aforesaid General has since run his whole Brigade (in the eagerness of Pursuit) into an Ambuscade losing all his Prisoners and nearly 200 of his own Men, I should not be much surprised to hear that Ld Wellington had recommended him to the Secretary of State for the Home Department, as an Officer whose consumate Skill and Abilities could nowhere be so well employed as in checking the unbridled efforts of King Ludd and his murderers.[2]

On the 1st June we once more left Cabeço de Vide and on the 11th were encamped on the Banks of the Agueda about 3 Miles from Cd Rodrigo. On the 12th Ld Wellington reviewed all the Cavalry and on the 13th his whole Army crossed the Agueda in three Columns, our Brigade with the Left under Genl Picton. On the 16th we arrived in front of Salamanca, where the Cavalry had a smart Skirmish. On the 17th the French having retired, our Troops entered Salamanca and invested a Fort which contained about 700 French. On the 19th the French Army under Marmont again made their appearance and cannonaded the King's Own Dragoons for some Time, which I am happy to state they stood with the greatest Firmness. Our Loss was confined to the Horses, 7 of which were killed and many of which were wounded. The French hovered about for some Days with the Idea of Relieving their Fort and at length finding themselves baffled in all directions and not liking to risk a Battle, the whole retired on the 26th and the Fort surrendered on the 28th, the Garrison consisting of 600 Men and upwards.

All the Cavalry have more or less experienced the skill of their Artillery Men but none so effectually succeeded in checking the approach of the Army towards Salamanca as Genl Bock's Brigade of Heavy Germans who singly, and unsupported, opposed themselves to Fort, Horse and Artillery and completely succeeded in keeping them in check until our Infantry had crossed the River and taken up their Positions.

The Fort, which at first was supposed to be very weak, stood a Siege of Ten Days and repulsed our Troops once, and had they been inclined to hold out, I do not see how it was possible to storm it. Our Fire had done little or no Damage to the Works but having set the Convent in Flames the Garrison were fearful of their Magazine blowing up.[3]

From Castelo Branco to Salamanca we were encamped every Night and as the Weather was remarkably fine the whole March, we found our Tents full as comfortable as the Portuguese Houses; from Ciudad Rodrigo to within six Miles of Salamanca the Road passes through a most Beautiful Forest of very rich Land with moving Grass up to the Horses' Knees, and as our mode of encamping is merely tying up the Horses to the largest Trees, a Camp of Cavalry in this Country is as pretty a Scene as it is ugly in England.

We are now, and have been for some days past, in a very decent Village in Rear of the Position and should be more comfortable were we not roused at Two O' Clock every Morning in order to be at the Alarm Post before Day Break, from whence we return as soon as a Report arrives from the outposts that all is Quiet. We have had a slight touch of the out Post Duty, which is truly Luxurious—no Trumpets, Baggage or Tents, our Backs to lie on and Bellies to cover us, without ever taking Saddles off the Horses even for the Purpose of cleaning, not to mention the Sun at noon Day in a Country as bare of shelter as Salisbury Plain. We are, however, better off than the Infantry who are exposed to the same Weather on a high Hill and consequently farther from both Wood and Water, neither of which is to be had nearer than two miles.

For three Days the Armies were within cannon Shot and the Videttes close to each other, the whole expecting an Engagement daily. The French have now fallen back on Zamora, where, I suppose, we shall follow as soon as Ld Wellington receives a Reinforcement of 4,000 British, the heavy Dragoon remounts and some Portuguese Infantry, all of which will arrive in two Days.

Salamanca is situated in an open Country completely bare of trees but is in some Respects superior to Oxford, notwithstanding the horrid Depredations of the French who have destroyed two Thirds of the Colleges and Convents in order to fortify their Convent.[4] The Cathedral, Square and some of the Colleges are the most Beautiful Buildings I ever saw, and not being exposed to severe Frosts or Smoaky Chimnies, are as fresh and the Sculpture as entire as ever. I should conceive that Three of their Colleges were larger than Christ Church but the Quadrangles much smaller. Their Cathedral is truly magnificent both within and without, not so long as ours usually are, although richer in Sculpture. It had a very narrow escape of being demolished with the other Churches etc., but Marmont was graciously pleased to save it on condition of the Clergy paying a pretty severe contribution. The Cathedral was threatened as often as the French wanted Money.

The People here are in every Respect superior to those we have seen in the South and certainly more zealous in the cause. Dons Julian [Sanchez] and Carlos [de España], the great Guerilla Leaders, joined our Army with their Myrmidons and a more verminous looking set of fellows you never beheld. The Infantry [are] in English Clothing and the Cavalry, both Horse and Man, completely armed and equipped in the Spoils of the Enemy, so that it is next to impossible to distinguish Friend from Foe. The Don himself wears a Pelisse like the 16th Dragoons with an immense Hussar Cap and the Eagle of Napoleon reversed. In this dress, accompanied by two aides de camp equally *genteel* in Appearance, Twelve Lancers, a Trumpeter in scarlet on a grey Horse and three led Horses I saw the renowned Chieftain enter Salamanca amidst the acclamations of the Multitude who received him with every mark of Respect.

The Dammage we have done the Inhabitants by Feeding our Cattle of every Description on Green Wheat is incalculable, but they appear to bear it with the greatest Patience, being perfectly satisfied that Lord Wellington will drive the French out of Spain.

Marmont withdrew behind the Douro on 1 July. Wellington moved up to the river, in expectation of support from the Galician army which had been ordered to attack Astorga and overrun the plains of northern Leon.

William continued his letter from Nava del Rey a week later.

General Graham left the Army for England on 6 July. Perceval, the Prime Minister, was assassinated by a madman in the Houses of Parliament on 11 May 1812.

Nava del Rey,
July 4th 1812.

This Afternoon I have an opportunity of forwarding this Letter towards England and shall therefore employ the Morning in endeavouring to fill upon the Sheet my Adventures up to the present Moment, but we have lately led such a wandering Life that I have some difficulty in recollecting dates and Places.

On the 27th—not the 28th—of June the Fort at Salamanca was taken and on the 29th our Brigade together with the whole Army advanced towards Toro but in the course of the day changed our direction and encamped in a Wood on the Valladolid Road, about one League and a half from where we started, having loitered about in the Sun 14 *Hours*. The next day we advanced about 4 Leagues and again encamped on the Downs, and on the first of July the whole Army amounting to 40,000 then encamped on the Banks of the Rio del Nava, about 6 Miles in rear of this Village, and the next Morning advanced as far as the Banks of the Douro, where the advanced Troops had some skirmishing and took a few Prisoners, but the whole of Marmont's Troops passed the River and blew up the Bridge without farther Molestation. Yesterday the 3rd Division, our Brigade, Don Julian's Cavalry and some Artillery proceeded to a Ford where our Artillery and theirs had some shots at each other, part of our Riflemen [of 60th Ft.] getting across the River and skirmishing but nothing consequential took Place. We were ordered back to this Town and once more got into decent Houses and good Beds, from whence I was again unnecessarily roused at 2 O' Clock, eat an enormous Breakfast and finding it to be a false alarm again retired to my downy Couch. The Third Division are still at the Ford but nothing will be attempted this day or we should not be indulged with a Halt.

The Douro is nearly half a Mile Broad and the Fords completely commanded by their Artillery, which are placed very advantageously on the opposite Banks so high that our Cannon cannot dislodge them, therefore some other place must be found or we shall never get to Valladolid. We are about equal to them in Numbers and the Deserters say they are famished for want of Bread.

From Salamanca to the Douro and from hence as far as the Eye can reach you can scarcely see a Tree, except the wood where we encamped on the 29th. The whole country is one extensive Range of Corn or Vines, the Villages are very large and the Roads remarkably good. The Harvest is now getting [in] fast and as the Commissary General has given an order for nothing to be brought from the Rear but Bread and Spirits, there appears to be every reason for expecting a long Business. The Troops are in the highest possible Spirits and astonishingly healthy.

The current Reports (I suppose Lyes) are that General Hill is advancing on Soult, who is supposed to have raised the Siege of Cadiz and retired towards Madrid. If this is true, Gen[l] Hill will have his own Division of 18,000 Men encreased to 28,000 by the Garrison of Cadiz being released, which, with the addition of Ballasteros' Force, will make him considerably stronger than Soult.[5] Another Report is that ten Thousand British have landed in Catalonia and laid siege to Barcelona,[6] and that the Galician Army, hitherto immovable for want of Transport, have advanced as far as Zamora, which will enable us to cross the Douro immediately.[7] If these Acc[ts] prove true, the Tide of Fortune appears to be turning against the French in every Direction. I am sorry to add that General Graham suffers so much from Weak Eyes, that his return to England is absolutely necessary—an event which L[d] Willington and the Army at large have great Reason to regret, especially at this Moment. If anything happens to the Peer, the Command of the whole Army devolves on Sir S. Cotton.[8]

I have received yours of the 27th May and Lucy's of 21st, together with Newspapers up to the Ninth of June, by which I am extremely rejoiced to find that in spite of every Effort, the Perceval Administration still continue to conduct the Reins of Government.

My Horses are still in good condition and the little Bay Mare rolling in Fat which cannot be wondered at, as we walk into a Barley or Wheat Field and out as much as we please.

Be kind enough to give my Love to my Mother, Brothers and Sisters and believe me Your dutiful Son, WILLIAM BRAGGE.

P.S.

The day before our Army left Salamanca, high Mass was performed and the Te Deum sung in the Cathedral and a splendid Ball given to the Allies in the Evening. Yesterday and today we have had some Rain but I trust it will prove fine tomorrow [or I] shall say nothing more of the Comforts of Campaigning.

[On Cover: JY 26 1812]

The next ten days were a time of watching and waiting for the first significant move to either Army. William wrote in the middle of the month describing this 'phoney' period.

Messrs. Cox and Greenwood were the Regiment's agents.

No. 18.   Pollos,
                                                  July 18th 1812.

My dear Father,

By some unaccountable Delay your Letter of the 8th June did not arrive until the 14th July, although we had received Letters and newspapers up to the 21st, but in the multiplicity of Business transacted solely by a Sergt in the Post Office at Lisbon, we cannot much wonder at a Letter or two occasionally lying idle.

I am extremely apprehensive from the Acct you give of my Vaiamonte Letter [of May 20th], that poor Bean will be disappointed in the Draft which I sent him, and in order to relieve him as soon as possible, I have by this Post written to him explaining the circumstance and requesting that in case other attempts fail, he would immediately apply to you, whom I have assured him will without delay procure him his Money. After having once experienced a Disappointment in procuring Money from England, it appears extraordinary that I should a second Time run my stupid Head into the same Gap, though I am not without a faint hope that my draft was drawn in that sort of way that Mr Stevenson (if I have written it so) will immediately inform the Bearer of the Probability of such a mistake.[9]

In order more effectually to prevent a recurrence of such Blunders on my part, I should be obliged to you to lodge a small sum in Mr Greenwood's Hands for my use, and request him to acquaint me of the circumstance, as most of the Officers transact money concerns with him, and would rather accept a Draft on

him than any other Banker. With regard to the Paymaster
General of the Army, [he] is now Four Months in Arrear and I
believe has no Money for the Pay of the Troops nearer than
Lisbon. Indeed if we were paid regularly as in England, I should
have very little occasion for troubling you.

I wrote to you a few Days back from Nava which is comparatively speaking a Heaven to this Village of Pollos, situated
immediately on the Banks of the Douro and about half a Mile
from the French Camp. The River is about half a Gun shot in
breadth and almost a continual succession of Fords, so that we
live in a State of alarm all Night and lie in Bed all Day. Our
Force consists of our own Reg^t and the third Division of Infantry
with about 4,000 Spanish Infantry and Don Julian's Guerillas,
who on the outpost Duty are very superior to any British Cavalry,
having the Fear of the Halter constantly before their Eyes.

For the first Day or two we lived here very peaceably and had
only a small Picquet out at Night, but as the French are expected
to cross the River in order to serve it out to Lord Wellington,
we are turned out bag and Baggage every Night at Ten, Breakfast on Beef and Onions at 4 in the Morning and afterwards
go to Bed until evening. Even this extraordinary sort of Life
agrees better with me than perfect inactivity and in an open
country without any source of amusement and a scalding hot
Sun, you cannot much wonder at a Person being little inclined
to take exercise voluntarily.

Marmont boasts of our having lost 3,000 Men in taking the
Fort at Salamanca (anglia 300)[10] and says he offer'd us battle for
three Days with little more than half our Force, which the British
Army cowardly refused, notwithstanding our superior position.[11]
He now gives out that in a few Days he crosses the River to
chastise us for our Temerity in advancing so far into Spain.

Lord Wellington, it is supposed, will not oppose his crossing
the River, and has actually fixed on a Position in rear of Nava
del Rey, where I sincerely hope Marmont will put the courage
and Skill of the British Army to the Proof in the course of a Day
or two. Our Forces are nearly equal, therefore after the brilliant
Examples of Talavera, Albuera etc., there can be no doubt as to
the Result of a General Engagement.

If Lord Wellington keeps his Men in their present Encamp-
ments, the being exposed Night and Day together with the

Heat of the Sun must destroy hundreds, and if Marmont suffers him to remain there a week longer, the Harvest will be under the Ground and out of reach of him—Marmont—and his Army, who will consequently suffer for the next three years a greater want of Bread than they do at present, which we know to be very great indeed.

Salamanca has suffer'd considerably since we left it by an explosion of Gunpowder, which Report says has destroyed 500 People and three Streets. It is, I fear, a melancholy Business though not so great an extent as reported.[12]

Our Remount arrived yesterday bringing a reinforcement of three subalterns, whose Assistance is greatly required as sickness and Staff Employment had reduced our original Number to five, which is no great Number for two Picquets a Night. The Horses were excellent and I do believe we are as well, if not better mounted than any Reg^t out here.

Like the Devonshire Huntsman, I have neither Butes or Breeches, everything coming from England having been left at Abrantes. If any one *ask* you to bring a Parcel for me, you may load him with a Map and Spy Glass, both of which I suffer from the want of and cannot procure here, unless the French were to retreat rapidly when I expect to make a number of Things. We have an honest depôt Seg^t at Belem who I know would send anything to me, if I could be certain of its ever getting to his Hands. Things sent by the Packet, I believe, come to a very considerable amount.

We have no Butter or Spirits and scarcely any vegetables but onions, therefore our meals are rather extraordinary—especially Breakfasts. Honey is nearly out as well as Cheese, therefore I almost pray for this Fight to be over, which will probably not be more dangerous than riding behind Old Major in your Buggy.

The French are very civil and allow us to water horses and bathe in the River; the latter experiment I have not tried although hundreds do every day.[13]

Be kind enough to give my Love to my Mother and Charlotte and accept the Same from Your dutiful Son,

WILLIAM BRAGGE.

I hope my next will be dated at Valladolid.

[On Cover: LISBON AU 2 1812]

After a feint to the west on the 15th, Marmont neatly side-stepped Wellington's Army, crossing the Douro on the night of 16-17 July. Sporadic fighting took place between the cavalry rearguard and the leading French units in the open country between the Trabancos and the Guareña rivers and the 3rd Dragoons were involved in a brisk engagement near Castrillo with a French brigade of dragoons attempting to outflank an Allied division. Thereafter Marmont manoeuvred so as to outstrip Wellington by hard marching hoping to catch him at a disadvantage. The latter, however, did not allow himself to become embarrassed and was prepared, if necessary, to fall back on Ciudad Rodrigo. Each was waiting for the other to make a mistake.

It was Marmont who faltered. On 22 July, Wellington seized his opportunity when the leading French division became dangerously strung out ahead of the remainder on the low hills south of Salamanca in the eagerness of outflanking the Allied right. The famous cavalry charge, led by Sir Stapleton Cotton and Le Marchant (who was killed in the moment of triumph) was the decisive factor in the Battle. Wellington commented: 'By God, Cotton, I never saw anything so beautiful in my life. The day is yours!'[14] It was all over in three hours.

William gave his impressions of the great Battle in a letter from Flores d'Avila written three days later, mentioning Le Marchant's death and also the gallant follow-up action of General Bock's German brigade at Garcia Hernandez. Le Marchant's charm and his able leadership in the field had evidently dispelled earlier fears of 'how very much Practice exceeds Theory' and his loss was keenly felt by a loyal admirer.

No. 19.

Flores d'Avila,
July 25th 1812.

My dear Father,

Knowing the Anxiety you and my Mother will feel upon hearing of a great and sanguinary Battle, in which the Third Dragoons bore no inconsiderable share, I take the earliest possible opportunity of informing you that I escaped perfectly sound, Wind and Limb, together with the Little Bay Mare who carried me through the Day delightfully and I believe to her Speed and Activity I may in a great measure attribute my marvellous escape, as I at one Time had to gallop along the whole Front of a French Brigade retreating in double quick step.

I have often heard you say, after reading the public Dis-patches, that you could never make anything of the History of a Battle, therefore I shall not attempt to describe the Fight of Salamanca any farther than what happened on our immediate Left and Right which was simply this. Marmont endeavoured to turn Lord Wellington's right and had taken possession of a Hill. [the great Arapile] in that direction but the British Hero rather counteracted his Intention by having detached the Third Div-ision still farther to the Right under General Packenham, with most of the Cavalry drawn up in Line on the Left of General Packenham, as if to keep up the communication between the Third Division and the rest of the Army. At least this was our situation about 3 O' Clock, the French keeping up a tremendous Cannonade on the cavalry and Infantry, our People not firing a Gun until Four, when I believe Lord Wellington gave the Signal for a general Attack by opening with six eighteen-Inch Howitzers.[15] Immediately upon this, our Right and Left turned theirs, the Enemy were driven from the Hills and the Cavalry advanced upon the Backs of the Infantry. Our Brigade literally rode over the Regiments in their Front [the leading brigade of Packenham's 3rd Division] and dashed through the Wood at a Gallop, the Infantry cheering us in all Directions. We quickly came up with the French Columns [Maucune's 5th Division] and charged their Rear. Hundreds threw down their Arms, their Cavalry ran away, and most of the Artillery jumped upon the Horses and followed the Cavalry. One or two charges mixed up the whole Brigade, it being impossible to see for Dust and Smoak, but this kind of Attack—so novel and unexpected—threw the French into confusion and gave our Infantry Time to get another Battle at them, when they served it out nicely, mak-ing them fly in all directions. We lost our General in a square of Infantry [the leading regiment of Brennier's 6th Division] and in him we have experienced a severe Loss. One Lieut. was killed by his side, but in other respects our Loss is trifling considering we were solely engaged with Infantry and Artillery. The Brigade marched off nine Pieces of Artillery and about 500 Prisoners.[16]

We marched to Alba de Tormes on the 23rd and here on the 24th (yesterday) and this day the whole Army halts. We passed by the Heavy Germans yesterday and saw the Ground where

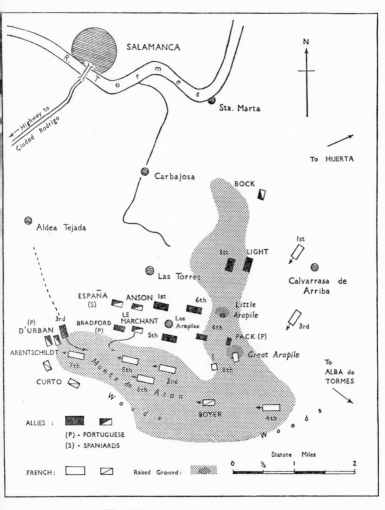

II. The Battle of Salamanca

they had gained immortal honour by charging three Squares of Infantry, breaking them and capturing 1,600 Prisoners. Lord Wellington was a Spectator and declares he never saw so gallant an Affair.[17]

Our Loss will, I should suppose, not exceed that at Badajoz. The French estimate theirs at 16,000; Lord Wellington certainly underrates it at 10,000. We know of 19 Pieces of Cannon and five Eagles taken besides Standards and Colours innumerable.[18] 7 French Generals were wounded, one taken Prisoner. Marmont had his arm amputated at Alba de Tormes and was conveyed from thence on a Litter borne by Twelve Grenadiers.[19] Sir Stapleton Cotton was wounded by the Portuguese.[20]

We have frequently been employed lately and on the 18th had the credit of saving the 1st [German] Hussars and the 14th from a perilous Situation, so that the Heavy Dragoons will, I trust, be in greater Repute than formerly.[21] The night before the action, we Bivouac'd close to Salamanca [at Santa Marta] and had scarcely linked Horses when a tremendous Clap of Thunder bursting over their Heads, the whole Brigade broke from their moorings and dashed over the Men, wounding about 50. The Night Dark, Rain in Torrents, French at Hand, and the Horses at Liberty in a Country as open as Salisbury Plain, only conceive our confusion. We recovered all our Nags but the 5th lost 18 Horses.[22] P.S. An acct has just arrived of the Death of Marmont, Bonnet and Marshal Beresford.[23]

You will receive this Letter nearly as soon as the Gazette Account, as it goes with the dispatches which are to be conveyed to England by Lord Clinton. You must excuse the writing for although 'sub Tegmine Tenti', I am not exactly 'lentus in Umbra'—in other words I lie down under a scorching Sun to write on a Blanket. Until last night I have not had my clothes off for a Fortnight and have seldom been under the cover of a tent but continue quite well.

We are on the high Road for Madrid, probably with a view of taking or making the French destroy their immediate Stores at Segovia.

With Love to all, Believe me Your dutiful Son,

WILLIAM BRAGGE.

VIII. The Battle of Salamanca.

From an acquatint in the collection of Col. Crookshank.

IX. Lieut.-General Sir Stapleton Cotton; later Field Marshal Viscount Combermere and Colonel Third Light Dragoons 1821–9.

From an engraving after a watercolour by T. Heaphy in the Cheylesmore collection.

(The original watercolour is in the possession of the Officer Commanding, the Queen's Own Hussars.)

P.S. What a Glorious Campaign this has been: —

Garrison of Badajoz	5,000
Do Ciudad	2,000
Fort at Salamanca	700
Taken at Almaraz	250
Llerena	150
	8,100
[SALAMANCA]	12,000
	20,000 approx.

The Spaniards know no bounds to their Joy. All the Medical People in Salamanca came out to dress the wounded and the most respectable Inhabitants carried the Soldiers on their Backs.

[On Cover: LISBON AU 15 1812]

The remnants of the Army of Portugal retreated through Valladolid to the North East, while King Joseph Bonaparte, who had been coming to help Marmont with 14,000 men, withdrew quickly to Madrid. Wellington was enthusiastically received at Valladolid on 30 July and within a week resolved to march on the capital. He could not pursue Clausel (who had succeeded Marmont) further without exposing his rear and he was keen to oust Joseph from Madrid or bring him to battle before he was reinforced by Soult. News had also reached him that a British force of about 8,000 men from Sicily under Gen. Maitland was hovering off the East coast to the distraction of Suchet. All in all the move seemed opportune, added to which the heartening effect throughout Europe of liberating the capital was no less significant.

Col. the Hon. William Ponsonby, who had commanded the 5th Dragoon Guards, succeeded Le Marchant in command of the brigade. Lord Charles Manners, formerly an A.D.C. to Lord Wellington, took command of the 3rd Dragoons from 8 August.

The Regiment was involved in a sharp encounter between El Escorial and Madrid in early August. It then formed part of Wellington's personal escort for his entry into Madrid, although William makes no mention of this in his next letter written from the capital.

No. 20.   Madrid,
                                                         August 18th 1812.

My dear Father,

After having halted one Day at the Village of Flores d'Avila,[24] we again proceeded with a burning scent after Marmont's Army but having allowed him too much Law, he got off without farther Molestation except the Loss of 900 Sick and some heavy Spanish Guns at Vallodolid,[25] where our Advance gave up the Pursuit. Our Brigade marched to the Banks of the Douro and the next Morning turned off for Segovia and Madrid, which latter Place we entered on the 12th August, having I believe loitered on the Road for that Purpose.

I did not obtain a Sight of Valladolid, which I very much regret as I wish to render this Campaign as much like a Tour of Pleasure as possible and by seeing as much as other People to prevent being humbugged hereafter. The Cathedral and Castle at Segovia were well worth seeing, as well as the magnificent Aqueduct built by Trajan. About two Leagues from thence we halted in a very Picturesque Valley amidst the Mountains of the Sierra Guadarrama, over which there is only one Pass but that so admirably contrived you may trot the whole way if your Horses are good enough. About a mile from this Encampment is the Royal Pallace of Ildefonso, a place much resembling our Hampton Court, but inferior to it in the size of the Apartments as well as in the Collection of Paintings with which the Rooms are crowded. The Gardens are magnificent but as we march there to take up our Quarters tomorrow, another Letter will probably give a better account of it.

Our next halt was near Escorial, where we were nearly Surprised by the French in consequence of the Portuguese Cavalry having run away in the most cowardly manner and in doing so upset 3 or 4 of our Light Guns which, together with some Gunners, Captain and 27 Horses were consequently taken by the Enemy. The heavy Germans, however, arrested their progress or they would have been in our Camp and taken half the Brigade.[26] Knight of 15th [Lt. Dr.] had just obtained a majority in the 11th Portuguese Cavalry which he joined two Days before this Affair (in which he narrowly escaped being taken) happened.

Of Lord Wellington's success and our very favourable Reception in Madrid you will have an account in the Newspapers. All the Prisoners marched out drunk, made the Escort drunk and then got wounded and plunder'd themselves in consequence.

The Inhabitants testified their Joy by hanging all their Curtains, Tapestry etc., out of the Windows, which had a very pretty effect and was greatly encreased for 3 Nights by a splendid Illumination with Immense Wax Candles. On the third Night they gave a Ball to the Army, which afforded me an opportunity of seeing more splendid Cloathes than I ever before saw. The Women are beautiful, very fond of the English and all—What d'ye call 'ems in England? Therefore you may suppose we rather regret leaving Madrid, although going to a Pallace.

Madrid is, I should suppose, the most delighted Metropolis in the World and certainly the best calculated for the Town Residence of a Gentleman, as there is in no Part of it those dreadful Nuisances which necessarily accompany many of our Trades in London and elsewhere. They have no Court end, but magnificent Houses scattered indiscriminately over the whole Town, many of them surpassing our best Houses. There is only one Royal Pallace, which although only in an unfinished State, still exceeds any we have in England. In short the Streets, Houses, Fountains and Public Walks are so good, as well as the Roads in the Neighbourhood, that I do think if any thing ever Tempts me out of England, it will be the Idea of spending a Winter at Madrid. There are no suburbs but each entrance to the Town passes under a beautiful Gateway.

The poorer Class have suffered dreadfully from the high Price of Provisions but I hope our Efforts will yet relieve them from their oppression. Bread has already fallen two Thirds in Price. Here, and at Salamanca, the 3 Shilling Loaf of two Pounds weight, being sold for one Shilling.

Adney informs me that Lucy is going to increase her Menagerie which I am sorry to hear. He likewise says his Team of Pointers is not so good in consequence of Phoebus beginning to grow old.

I fear Jack's Examination is a humbug, as being refused your Testimonium is what is in Oxford termed being *plucked*.

I have received two Letters lately, yours of the 27th July arrived yesterday. With regard to the Banker's Account, I am almost as much in the dark as yourself but can assure you I have only drawn two Drafts, one in favour of Mr Bean for 50£, and one in favour of Mr Sealy for 26£ odd. From Bean I have never heard, therefore trust his Draft is paid, and as for Mr Sealy, either he or Capt. Heywood owes me 100 Dollars which I sent by the letter to Lisbon. Heywood is now extremely ill at Celorico, therefore it will be some Time before I hear from him.

Pray give my Love to my Mother and Charlotte and Believe me Your dutiful Son, WILLIAM BRAGGE.

When I live in Madrid I will buy some better Paper.

[On Cover: LISBON SE 13 1812]

Wellington remained in Madrid until he had adequate information on Soult's movements. On the last day of August he heard that Joseph was still moving eastwards and he concluded that Soult was beginning to march in that direction as well. It was time to attend to the Army of Portugal again, which had recently re-occupied Valladolid.

The 3rd Dragoons left the capital after only a week there to return to San Ildefonso. Much as Madrid appealed to William, he must have been even more delightfully distracted here for his next letter fails to supply the promised description of the gardens and the 'French château, the antithesis of the proud, gloomy Escorial, on which it turns its back',[27] where the treaty effectively handing Spain over to France was signed in 1795 and where in later years more important events in the turbulent history of Spain were to take place. The gardens would have had greater appeal for William, though. These were, and still are, of outstanding beauty, covering some 350 acres on the slope opposite the Palace. Twenty-six fountains play in the grounds, the chief of which throws a jet over a hundred feet high and is easily visible from Segovia. After the scorched northern plains, the Promised Land indeed.

As William implies in his next letter, written from Valladolid after its re-capture, his stay at San Ildefonso was all too short before he was plunged back into the rough, hard life of active campaigning.

No. 21.   Valladolid,
                                                        8th Septr 1812.

My dear Father,

I have had a Letter ready written for some Days but as the Army has advanced pretty rapidly since I began it. I am induced to write it over again in order to give you the latest Intelligence and I understand the Packet leaves Vallodolid this Afternoon. An English Mail has arrived up to the 21st August but the Letters are not yet delivered.

We left Madrid on the 19th of August and in three Days reached the Royal Palace of Ildefonso, where I got into very excellent Quarters and for once spent a delightful Week in Spain, being constantly in the Company of a very Gentlemanly and entertaining Patron who was Vicar of the Place and had a very accomplished Niece living with him, as good natured as she was pretty, therefore you may suppose I was what the Spaniards call 'muy contento' with my situation. [This] was soon changed for one of a very different Nature, for at the end of the Week we were pushed on to the Villages near the Douro doing a sort of half outpost Duty which lasted another Week, when Lord Wellington brought up his Divisions and crossed the Douro at Herrera immediately to the great surprise of the French, who had no idea of his being nearer than Arevalo. They waited for us to attack them, but the Artillery having gone to the wrong Ford, it was found necessary to defer the Attack until the next Morning (yesterday). The Gentlemen, however, retired in the Night and blew up the Bridges [over the Pisuerga on the other side of the town], therefore we entered Valladolid (the most disaffected Town in Spain) without opposition.[28]

Lord Wellington is here with four Divisions and a devilish Temper in consequence of the Artillery not having come up in Time Yesterday, which circumstance saved the French from another beating, as we had as many Men as they. His Lordship had given an order to attack which was afterwards countermanded. The Enemy have retired towards Burgos, but not a Soul of the HeadQuarters Staff knows whether we shall follow them or return towards Madrid to assist Soult, who is advancing from the South spreading all over the country most direful Proclamations. When the latest Accounts left the South of Spain, Soult was at Cordoba and Genl Hill at Almaraz, therefore all is going on well in that Quarter.[29] And if one may venture to augur anything from Ld Wellington's countenance *previous* to his crossing the Douro, nothing could be more favourable than the present situation of our Affairs.

Amidst the Troubles of Spain some few English have remained in Madrid, amongst whom I got acquainted with a most curious

Trio: an Irish Friar, formerly confessor to the Queen, a Scotch Saddler and a mad Widow, all of whom have resided there upwards of 20 Years. I likewise met with several People who spoke English.

The Theatre of Madrid has degenerated in proportion with every thing else since the gay Days of Laura and Arsenia. At present the Company of Comedians are very paltry and the most applauded Actor amused us with using the Pot de Chambre and pulling off his Breeches, previous to going into Bed, which Scene concluded the Play.[30]

Sir Howard Douglas [the British Commissioner at Corunna] has just arrived from Corunna, where I believe he has been a sort of Agent for furnishing Spanish Armies with Arms etc. The Account he gives of the renowned Galician Army is really miserable, therefore we can reckon nothing on any assistance from them, and as for the Guerillas, I'll tell you a Story.

Some Time in May last, 800 of these formidable fellows undertook the Siege of Ildefonso, which was at that Time garrisoned by eighty of the Imperial Guard and two officers. 300 entered the Town and 500 surrounded the Place about Noon, but in less than two Hours the Eighty French drove them out of the Town killing and taking numbers, to the great satisfaction of the Inhabitants who have a greater dread of these Villains than they have of the French. My Patron and his Niece were Eye witnesses and told me this Anecdote.

I have this morning rec^d two Doubloons being a Fortnight's pay, and must of Necessity buy some Cloathes as every thing I have is worn out, and my new Boots are at Abrantes, where—I suppose—they will stay until the War is over. We have lately been in a state of Beggary but I trust we shall now get Money more regularly. Mr Sealy has given Heywood credit for the 100 Dollars I sent him in May so I hope to be rich some Day or other.

I hope to God this will be Lord Wellington's last Campaign in Spain as I get quite weary of Service. You cannot conceive half the Misery of it—we are wretched. What think ye of having choice of Quarters (in a Village where the People were half of them absolutely dying) after 5 Generals and their Staff? This happened to my Squadron the other Night and the consequence was that I slept in the same House with two other Officers, two

Portuguese Boys, the Patron and his wife and 9 Guerillas. I wish some of our gay young Men in England could have changed Beds for the Night. I forgot to observe there were *no Doors* in this elegant Hovel but plenty of Fleas.

We have not seen Lord Wellington's Dispatches in the English Newspapers but if the Portuguese is a literal Translation, our Brigade, and particularly our Reg^t, have no great reason to thank him for his commendation. On the 18th of July, the 3rd were ordered out in a hurry to support the 1st Hussars and 14th [Lt. Dr.] who at that Time were completely clubbed and running away, until a charge from the Third turned the Tide, which was done in sight of Lord Wellington and the whole Army. The Regiment afterwards kept their Ground with Riflemen shooting at them until our Infantry had Time to come up. Upon this occasion Genl Alten and Col. Hervey thanked Major Clowes and they in turn got thanked by his Lordship. On the 22nd [Salamanca] the Dragoons of our Brigade took 7 Guns, Horses and all to the Rear, and Prisoners out of Number—I should suppose certainly not less than 2,000—therefore we are rather vexed that Lord Wellington did not make mention of us more favourably in his Dispatches, which in England are read as Gospel. 5 of our Men had charge of 700 the whole Night.[31]

I have been nearly loosing the Bay Mare but she is now getting about again and is really an invaluable Creature on Service, being always fat and hearty.

The Artillery Officer taken near Madrid on the 11th Augt has made his Escape. He says the French begin to croak, saying it is all over with them in Spain. This Northern Army only mustered 22,000 yesterday which was six weeks since 45,000. With Maitland and Hill our Army must nearly equal theirs. Marshal Beresford brought up 4 different Brigades on the 22nd and was advancing a 5th Time about 20 yds in front of the Colours when a Ball struck him.

Give my Love to my Mother and Charlotte and believe me, Your dutiful Son, WILLIAM BRAGGE.

Claret is here 3d a Bottle. At Madrid the English drank up a stock for 6 *Months* in 3 Nights.

[On Cover: LISBON SE 29 1812]

Wellington followed the French to Burgos and beyond. By this time though, the vigour of the Allied advance had spent itself.

William wrote in the last week in September, describing the attempts to take the castle, which was being stoutly defended by a garrison of 2,000, and his own narrow escape on the 19th during a cavalry reconnaissance to find out how far the French had withdrawn.

No. 22.

Villayerna,
a Village one League
in front of Burgos,
Septr 25th 1812.

My dear Father,

We left Valladolid on the morning of the 10th and arrived in the Vicinity of Burgos about the 20th, the French not allowing us to make more than about Two Leagues a Day. The Armies encamped regularly within sight of each other, but the Enemy appeared not to have the slightest Inclination for a second Engagement, nor did our noble Leader wish to attack them as long as they would keep out of his Way.[32] They took up a very strong Position one morning in order to gain Time but decamped and retired through Burgos,[33] leaving a powerful Garrison in a very strong Castle, which—in my opinion—will cost the British Army dearer than Ciudad Rodrigo.

Our Troops succeeded in taking an outwork of the Castle the first Evening [19th], but not without considerable loss on our part, in consequence of Ld Wellington having employed a Division not used to the noble science of storming. Had the Light or Third Division been there [they were still at Madrid], we should not have lost above 50 Men, but as it was the Troops advanced to the Glacis and there stood to be shot at without endeavouring to gain the Fort, and have since that failed in an attempt on the Castle. I believe the Army would regret their Loss more had they not foolishly complained to Lord Wellington after the 22nd [July—Salamanca] of not having 'Justice done them'—anglia: not fighting enough—to which his Lordship replied: 'They had been very ill used but he would see them righted at the first opportunity', which unfortunately happened to be the Fort and Castle of Burgos. The Division is composed of Guards and Highlanders.[34] I am happy to say we marched in rear of the whole Army and had consequently nothing to do the whole Journey, which was upon the whole the most unpleasant we have had, it being extremely cold and the Nights very wet, but the Weather is now warmer and I trust we shall have no more Rain, which is certainly a curse to Soldiers.

By our Batteries not having opened yet, I rather think we are endeavouring to take the Castle by Sap,[35] which is—I believe—rather a tedious process, but as Lord Wellington in all his military Career never missed taking a Fort, I do not imagine he is going to be outdone at Burgos. The French have a strong Position about 8 Leagues from here, but will hardly advance to relieve their Garrison. Their Troops are certainly in a great state of Insubordination and are so strongly impressed with the Idea of *going to France* that another Battle would prove fatal to the army of Portugal. They have one strong Fort between this and the Ebro [at Miranda] and another at Pamplona.

All the Troops, both English and French, are considerably weakened by Sickness; our sick amount to 20,000, in which are included all men taking Medicine whether with or away from their Regiments, and the Army under Soult are so weakened by it, that he is striving to the utmost to keep out of Gen¹ Hill's Road.[36]

The noted Galician Army have at length joined us under Castaños and look much like an Army of Mendicants with Brown Cloaks on. Their Artillery are very superior to the French and are in general drawn by English Horses with a complement of Men mounted on the best Spanish Nags. They have one squadron of Hussars dressed in the same style with ours but the rest of their cavalry are inferior to Don Julian's Guerillas. I believe their effective strength does not exceed 10,000.

I was very much delighted to find that my Letter had anticipated the Gazette of the 22nd [July], and care not how soon I have the Pleasure of communicating such another glorious piece of News. I see the opposition Papers do not give Lord Wellington credit for some of his Laconic Speeches previous to the Battle, but although not the Language of the Marlboroughs and Peterboroughs, it is very much this modern Hero's style of addressing his Generals and is found to answer equally well.

The Parcel you sent Cartwright for me is, I have no doubt,

perfectly safe, at *Abrantes* where our necessaries are likely to remain, tho' Report says everything is coming up. I think the Contest will end in Spain as our Army is here maintained at nearly one Third the Expense in consequence of the abundance of Corn.

Our present Leader (Col. Ponsonby) is no great Gen[l]. He was ordered the other Day to advance until he was stopped, which he did by moving our Reg[t] down an Avenue with a Front of Threes and no advanced Guard until the Enemy thought proper to Fire a Gun, which enfiladed the Road and might have killed 30 Men had it been pointed properly. Another shot took two Light Dragoons Heads off and the next passed under my Mare's legs and the covering Serg[ts]' horses without doing either any Injury.

Burgos is one of the worst large Towns I have seen in Spain and the Country round it extremely dreary although abounding with Corn. The People [are] horridly ugly and what is rather remarkable for Spaniards excessively dirty, therefore I have no wish to go farther North, except to embark.

I still continue well, but most of our Officers are complaining and some of them very ill of Fevers and Agues which cannot be much wondered at as we have only been under a Roof two Nights since we left Valladolid.

Be kind enough to give my Love to my Mother, Brothers and Sisters and accept the Same from, my dear Father, your dutiful Son, WILLIAM BRAGGE.

Remember me kindly to Froward the first Time you see him, and tell him how much obliged I am to him for forwarding my Salamanca Letter.

I thank you for lodging Money for me with Greenwood, some of which I hope to transfer immediately.

It was during the siege of Burgos castle that Wellington noticed the deteriorating morale of the Portuguese and the diminishing energy of the British soldiers, blunted by staleness, sickness and the fatigue of long marches.

The castle had been mined unsuccessfully in several places. One mine was still to be sprung. Throughout the whole siege Wellington had been severely handicapped by the lack of guns and ammunition, since his heavy siege train had been sent back to Ciudad Rodrigo just before the battle of Salamanca and had never been called forward again.

The apparent stalemate continued. Meanwhile the well-being of the Allied army was further tried by cold, wet, gloomy weather which swept across the bleak encampment.

William described the dismal circumstances in mid-October but was glad to tell his father that he was no longer short of cash in the same letter.

Parliament was prorogued at the end of July. Astorga fell to the Galicians on 18 August. Morton Pitt had been an M.P. for Dorset since 1789; his only daughter, the Countess of Romney, had just died.

No. 23.

Villayerna,
3 Miles from Burgos,
Octber 18th 1812.

My dear Father,

Since the commencement of the Year 1812, I do not believe you have ever received two Letters from me at the same Village, nor would that event have now happened had not Lord Wellington been under the Necessity of keeping a strong Force in the immediate Neighbourhood of Burgos, in consequence of the Difficulty of reducing the Garrison in its Castle which the Enemy have threatened to relieve more than once, although their Efforts have hitherto been shabby in the Extreme.

From the Moment we first invested this cursed Castle, the Weather has proved particularly unfavourable to our operations, having scarcely ceased raining the whole Time accompanied by occasional High Winds and very severe Nights, notwithstanding which our Divisions of Infantry still remain encamped and may truly be said to resemble 'Father Pigs', not having any covering but very indifferent Huts built of Boughs and open at each end, without any Straw, Palliasses or things of that nature to lie on. You can easily conceive the state of such a Camp on low Ground after three Weeks Rain, which has almost filled our Trenches with Mud and Water as well as the Camp. Our Men for the last Fortnight have had a Lodgement on the outer Wall of the Castle from whence they keep up an incessant Fire of Musquetry but I fear without doing the Enemy any farther Mischief than preventing their annoying our Working Parties. The Castle is now mined in several Places and I expect we shall make a desperate attempt either this Evening or Tomorrow Morning as his Lordship's Dispatches ought to go off the next Day.[37] At the beginning of the Fray we had Thunder, Lightning and Nelson (3 eighteen Pounders so-called) to assist us, but the contending elements have long since given way to the superior skill of the immortal Nelson, who now singly, opposes himself to nine Twenty Four Pounders.[38]

I received yours of the 12th September a few Days since and this Morning had a Letter of the 15th from Greenwood acknowledging the receipt of 100£ which you were good enough to lodge in his Hands for my use. I have not seen Newspapers of a much later Date but understand that Lord Wellington has some which announce the Dissolution of Parliament, as well as a Truce between the Russians and French, a Piece of Intelligence which although extremely probable I shall be sorry to see confirmed, as with the Assistance of Russia I am thoroughly convinced we could settle the French in this Part of the world, whereas a strong Reinforcement from France might easily turn the Tables on us.

The Spaniards according to their own accounts have been doing wonders lately, but I am incredulous enough not to believe a single Syllable of their Dispatches. They starved the French out of Astorga and accepted *their own* proposals for a Capitulation, but had no sooner got possession of the French than they disarmed the Escort (1 Frenchman to Five Spaniards) stripped both men and Officers, and marched the whole to *Corunna* to be exchanged at a convenient opportunity. The First and second-in-commands shot themselves the next Day and the Spaniards used the remainder as ill as possible on the Road; but villainous as it is, the French richly deserve this treatment. The Spanish Armies put one in mind of the Foppish Midshipman who marked his ownly Two shirts 59 and 60.

It must be allowed that War, or rather Service, is a famous thing for promotion. I was twelfth Lieutenant when I landed at Lisbon; am now Fifth and shall probably be first for purchase by the Time I have served the regular Period as more of our Capts and Subs are heartily sick of the Business.[39] As a preliminary step to promotion, I should like to know how much my Freehold would sell for, as I should wish it to go for that purpose.

The dissolution of Parliament happening so soon after Mr M. Pitt's severe domestic calamity will probably induce him not to offer himself again for the county,⁴⁰ in which case I suppose there will be a union of Colours, having myself no hopes for the King of Basan, who Lord Charles [Manners] says: 'We (meaning the Brothers Hunt) have considered a Poor Creature since his Marriage and fond of Money.'⁴¹

With the Assistance of borrowed Money and some deceased Officers' Kits, I have been enabled to rigg myself again tolerably well but was a few weeks since almost naked. This Climate certainly has agreed with my constitution wonderfully well hitherto, and will I hope continue to do so. I am become immensely heavy and Fat, and shall have a very respectable Bay Window by the Time I return to England, which I trust we shall do before another Twelve months pass over our heads.

Do you not think it very bad Policy to send Life Guardsmen on service and to keep Hussars in London, who are in no respect half so well calculated to keep Cockneys in order as the Old London Troops? I begin to think with the Editor of the *Examiner* that some Princes were born for Tailors.

My horses are at present in excellent condition and so indeed are most of the Troopers, except the Old ones, who at this Time of Year always look miserably ill. We have had a Field Day, a Review and two false Alarms since we came to this Village. I find, by referring to a Journal, that this is the only Instance of our having remained Three Weeks in the same Place since January. Should this Castle be taken, we shall certainly go back to the South of Spain, which is a much pleasanter Part of the World to be in, as the People in this Neighbourhood are poor and almost all of them Labourers.

I am sorry to have so indifferent an Account of Jack and would willingly write him a Letter did I not know that most of his Friends had taken that trouble in vain. I wish for a week or two he could see the Luxury of being an Infantry Officer on Service, whose Life is many Degrees worse than that of the meanest mechanic in England, but 'He that is truly dedicate to War, Hath no self Love'.

Ned Phelips suffers very much from the Ague. He has now been ill more or less for three Months; if he gets better one Day, he is out coursing the next—how like Papa.

With this, you ought to have received Five Letters from me since the Battle; one from Flores d'Avila, one from Madrid, Valladolid and Burgos. I have sent as many to the Adneys but do not get so many answers from them as I could wish.

I hear every Gun that is fired against the Castle and believe the Firing to have encreased greatly since Yesterday Morning. The Castle is situated much like that at Corfe, but the Twenty Four Pounders on its Top command the opposite Hill, which could not have been the case at Corfe Castle. There appears to be a Triple Line of Defence.

The Ground is so slippery and dirty that walking is almost impossible. I shall therefore ride out in the rain in order to cure a Heavy cold.

I wish you to remember me to old Fowler, who will I hope live to see me come back again. Do you think he and his Family would stand cannonading well?

With Love to my Mother, Sisters and Brothers, Believe me my Dear Father, Your dutiful Son, WILLIAM BRAGGE.

[On Cover: PACKET LETTER PLYMOUTH]

On 21 October Wellington realized that there was no purpose in further operations at Burgos. He had learned from Hill the day before that Soult and Joseph had joined forces and were advancing from the south with about 60,000 men, placing him in an awkward position. There was no alternative but to fall back and order Hill to meet him on the Tormes. The two corps were united on 8 November with hardly the loss of a man.

The withdrawal had its eventful moments. By bad staff work Ponsonby's brigade was ordered to fall back by a lone mountain road from Burgos, thereby being out of touch with the rest of the Army when the French seized a bridge ahead of their route on 23 October. Fortunately the Brigade managed to slip through undetected.

Soult put his army across the Tormes on 14 November but thereafter he was much too cautious and Wellington extricated the Allied army and retired to the Agueda. As he described it, 'he got clear in a handsome manner of the worst scrape he was ever in'.[42]

The Army reached Ciudad Rodrigo four days later having suffered dreadful hardships and privations on the way. With some remarkable lack of understanding, the supplies from Salamanca were routed back through two villages twenty miles north of the main

route. This was largely due to the incompetence of the Quartermaster General, Sir Willoughby Gordon, of whom more will be
heard. The orderly retirement degenerated into a hunger-striken
body struggling urgently towards the safety of the Portuguese frontier. Many believed that by some cruel chance the French had gained
a bloodless victory. The well-established, familiar winter quarters
behind the Agueda were a welcome sight.

A rather dejected, crestfallen William wrote to his father when
the ordeal was over.

Sir Edward Paget relieved Graham as Wellington's Second-in-
command. Major Clowes's application for resignation was accepted a
few days before William's letter was written. Caffarelli commanded
the French Army of the North, which helped the Army of Portugal
push Wellington away from Burgos.

No. 24.   Aldeia da Ponte,
                                         Novr 26th 1812.

My dear Father,

I perfectly agree with you in thinking it a most secondary
Consideration whether a Person dates his Letters from a Pallace
or a Pigstye, provided he enjoys the same State of Health in
both Situations, but I very much doubt whether there would not
be a visible difference in two Letters written by the same Person
from 'Butye's' Cabin and the Bedford Coffee House. I am led to
make this Remark from an Observation in your last Letter that
mine from Valladolid and Madrid contradict each other, a circumstance which I can only attribute to the Badness of my
Quarters, Toughness of the Rations or a short Allowance of
Rum, as I still mean to maintain that Madrid is the most
delightful City, and Ildefonso the most beautiful Valley, I ever
saw in my Life. With regard to the rest of Spain, it is equally
ugly and uninteresting to the English Traveller, having scarcely
any Meadows or Trees except here and there a sombre Forest of
Pines.

You will already have seen a circumstantial Account of our
late Retreats, which have really been very Disastrous and from
want of a little better Arrangement in the Commissariat and other
Departments rendered more terrible than a Sanguinary Action,
as besides the Inclemency of the Weather we had the worst of all
Enemies to contend with, proving fatal to Hundreds, namely
Hunger and want of Spirituous Liqour, no Rations being given

to the Troops for Four—and in many Instances Six—Days. The Weather was very Rainy, intensely cold, and the Country we had to retreat over much like part of Oxfordshire, being very deep and intersected by numberless Brooks and Rivers which in our Advance to Salamanca we never perceived. Our Spring Waggons and Mules went by one Road and the Troops by another, so that every knocked up and wounded Man fell into the Enemies Hands and all the Cavalry went with the same column of Infantry, leaving two others completely uncovered. To this circumstance we owe the loss of Sir E. Paget [on 17th Novr] and Quantities of Baggage. Sir Edward was taken between two Columns of our Infantry retiring on the same Road and immediately recognised by a French Dragoon who recollected him in Egypt.[43]

After being kicked about for a Month without any Hopes of Reversing oneself on these Rascals, I cannot say but that I felt considerable Satisfaction at being once more across the Agueda and secure from all Alarms, but I regret excessively having been obliged to have to recourse to this measure, which has disappointed the Expectations of England and the Hopes of Spain, besides which they will revert into a State of Despondency and never again have any Confidence in the Effort of a British Army. It has likewise given our Enemies an opportunity of exulting, which I could have dispensed with, though they certainly have brought all their Troops from the farthest Points of Spain to effect (by Manoeuvre and not by fighting) this desirable object. I must give the French Credit for having once more outmanoeuvred the English in the passing of a River, over which they threw Ten Thousand Men before we were aware of it. Having got their Troops over, they declined a second Contest on the Arapiles but proceeded in the direction of Ciudad, necessarily compelling us to retire. Had they procrastinated passing the River another Day, Salamanca would still have beeen ours.[44]

The Situation of Spain is truly pitiable, being constantly exposed to the Ravages of three Roving Armies and the Inhabitants sure to suffer either in Person or in Property, let them enlist under which Banner they will. We deceive them, the French impoverish them and the Spanish Troops, regular and irregular, plunder them of every earthly Thing they possess. Of the Spanish Troops I still entertain the same opinion which is, that they

X. An extract of William Bragge's letter of 23 May 1813.

(See pages 99–100)

XI. Major-General the Hon. William Ponsonby.

From an engraving by G. Maile.

will not stand Fire unless greatly superior in Numbers; but allowances are certainly to be made for Men dragged from their Homes, without confidence in their Officers, without Pay, without regular Rations and but for the Liberality of England, would be without clothing. Amongst their Leaders there are undoubtedly some very Brave Men, but generally speaking they want even that good Quality and either from Jealousy, Peculation or Treason are little worthy of their Situations. Ballasteros, for disrespect of Lord Wellington, and Don Carlos for Peculation are both in arrest and superceded.[45]

During the late Operations our usual good luck has attended me, and the Brigade I belong to; me in having escaped throughout the Campaign without Pip or Palsy, which is rather to be wondered at, as I never changed my Clothes or washed my Face and Hands for the last 6 Days, and the Brigade in having no Fighting when in the Rear and escaping annihilation in the late March to Valladolid when completely cut off from the rest of the Army by 5,000 French Cavalry with a River in our Rear, through which we accidentally found a Ford in the Night. Nor must I forget a liberal supply of Pigs, Beef and Mutton, which the Heavy Germans had shot and left in the Camp upon being suddenly ordered out when we were without Rations.[46]

We were in this Village last January when it did not afford us a Mouthful of Forage, in which respect it is now considerably bettered, but having since that Period received the Benefit of an *eighth* Visit from the French [it] is in a most Dilapidated State and has very few Houses remaining with Roofs on, notwithstanding which we have at present Two Portuguese Regts of Infantry, a Squadron of Dragoons and Troop of R.[oyal] W.[agon] Train or (as I see on the opposite Wall) Newgate Blues. We expect to move to Fundão tomorrow or the next Day.

So great has been the Mortality amongst our Officers, that I have been very apprehensive of having a Junior Lieut. put over my head in consequence of my not having served Three Years; but as one of our Captains has lately changed his mind, I am tolerably secure until May. The Army List should now run: Shakespear [A.D.C. to Sir S. Cotton], *Burn*, Bowater—Adj., Bragge, leaving me fourth on the List and second for purchase. Major Clowes having resigned goes home tomorrow. In him we have a great Loss.

G

One of your Letters reached me at Dueñas, and two others here, together with one from Adney informing me of Lucy's Dissappointment. Should it be attended with no farther serious consequence than the Loss of a Nephew for a Twelvemonth, I shall be very happy. Adney's Letter is chiefly about his Dogs and Horses which are usually superexcellent.

In consequence of Bean's directing his Letter to a Confidential Serg^t, I did not receive it until two Months after its arrival. He duly received his money from Stephenson and I have lately recovered mine from Sealy, which has made me tolerably rich to begin the Winter Sports. My horses, from the severity of the Weather during the last month and want of Corn, are wasted to nothing, especially the Dun Mare who the last Morning was from the above reason completely knocked up. She is so big and so liable to a *Fever in the Feet,* that I should certainly sell her could I find a Purchaser.

It rained till we reached this Village. Since that, it has been a hard Frost and will apparently Tomorrow be a deep Snow. I and my Captain are in a Room, with a Roof to it and out of pure Charity made room for two Field Officers to sleep by moving the Table and Chairs.

Whilst in position near Salamanca, we heard of Caffarelli's having retired to Burgos. He made a Feint that way, but speedily turned down the Douro, and would have crossed and been in our rear had not our Army retreated.[47]

I do not think the French have too much reason to boast of the Year 1812, in which they have lost 50,000 Men and are at last obliged to bring all their Troops to one point. I trust my Lord will breed more Mischief this Winter.

With Love to my Mother, Brothers and Sister, Believe me Your Dutiful Son, WILLIAM BRAGGE.

Disappointing though the outcome of the campaign of 1812 may have appeared in terms of visible conquests, it had none the less been a severe blow to the French. In spite of reinforcements, they were weaker at the end of November than in March by 30,000. One French General wrote later: 'Lord Wellington has retired unconquered with the glory of the laurels of Arapiles, having restored to the Spaniards the country south of the Tagus and made us destroy our magazines, our fortifications—in a word all that we

have gained by our conquest, and all that could assure the mainten-
ance of it.'[48]

The regiments dispersed to various cantonments to make good the
ravages of the last days of the retreat. For many weeks to come,
about a third of the Allied army was on the sick list as typhus and
dysentery ran their course. Officers and men alike of the 3rd Dragoons
fared no better than any other regiment, but William seems to have
led a charmed life through this distressing period.

On 29 November the Regiment marched via Guarda to Seixo,
where it remained until the end of December. William wrote his last
letter of the year from there on Christmas Eve.

The Life Guards arrived at Lisbon on 23 November after a very
rough passage. Wellington left for Cadiz on 12 December to try and
persuade the Cortes to reorganize the Spanish Army commands
and the country's administration. Much of what he asked for was
granted.

No. 25.   [Seixo,]
                                                  Dec[r] 24 1812.

My Dear Father,

This side of the Paper was fully intended for my brother
Champniss, who has lately written me a long and amusing
Letter, but yours of the 26th Nov[r] having arrived on the 20th
Instant, I was induced to postpone sending Charlotte's Letter to
the Post and differ writing to Champ until another opportunity.

I was extremely happy to hear that you had got one of your
young Horses *so far* on the Road to Church, and trust that with
the Assistance of a sharp curb and a new Point or two, they will
both trot quickly to the Church Hatch before I have the pleasure
of seeing them again. I have lately met with a little Preferment
myself, which—the Paymaster informs me—will encrease my
Pay and Allowances (or rather the latter) nearly 100£ per
annum, should I hold the Appointment so long, which is the
command of Heywood's Troop, who is gone to England on a
Matrimonial Scheme and is not likely to return.

Since I last wrote to you, the Dun Mare has given me a Devonshire Roll but without hurting me or her own Knees, but I immediately resolved to sell her and have in the mean Time given
a lot of Money for a Mare of Heywood's, which has been the
Admiration of every Body ever since he had her. She is [a] five
Year Old and was bred by his Father, and is I firmly believe

really valuable, tho' I should not have ventured upon so high a Price in England; but in this Country, where you take into consideration the Difficulty of getting a Horse out, the uncertainty of his standing the Work and [the] Probability of his not pleasing you when he does, you may pay a few Pounds more in consequence.

I yesterday received a Letter from Col. Clowes [his promotion was effective from 17th Aug. 1812], dated Lisbon, who informs me the Blues are looking beautifully but the Life Guards are in a wretched state; the Horses out of Condition, the Officers for the most part tired of Service and determined to send in their resignations and the Men in a *State of Mutiny*. As I am not aware how far he is in earnest, I do not wish you to communicate this last piece of intelligence to any Army Man; but if at any Time you can inform me that a London Mob have stoned the Hussars out of Piccadilly and made the Prince recall his Life Guards, I shall have additional Satisfaction in receiving your Letter.

It was fine Yesterday, but rain again to Day. The Mountains are covered with Snow but we still sit with the Shutters open in a Room without a Fire and do not experience any great Inconvenience from the Cold. We must draw nearer to Coimbra in a few Days and I shall probably have an opportunity of seeing Oporto during the Winter. I hope to commence the next Campaign with a better set out than I did last Time and fully intend swapping my Portuguese Valet for a man who can frighten the Ration Beef as well as clean Boots. By this means I shall live more comfortably at nearly the same Expense, and my Dragoons will only have to attend to their Horses.

We have a reinforcement of Officers, Men and Ninety Horses at Belem. This is the Third Remount this Year. They continue sending out 3 Horses to one man and one third of the Nags fail in consequence. Lord Wellington is gone to Cadiz with two Officers of his Staff only. The French have only one very small corps in Salamanca and the Vicinity. Their Advanced Posts are one League on this Side of the Town.

Wishing you all a merry Xmas and happy New Year, I remain, my Dear Father, Your Dutiful Son,

WILLIAM BRAGGE.

26 Decr: We march on the 28th to a decent Town on the Road to Coimbra. The Little Mare slipt a Foal at Guarda.

CHAPTER FOUR

Portugal to the Pyrenees

January 1813–August 1813

At the end of December, the 3rd Dragoons marched to Arganil, where they had been quartered a year before. There they gradually regained their strength.

William wrote in the first week in February, admitting the loss of his best horse and summarizing very clearly the local resentment of the publication in the English Press of Wellington's Memorandum to senior officers after the retreat from Burgos.

In common with many other officers, William had little good to say for Sir Willoughby Gordon, whose professional inefficiency was extremely embarrassing in the Peninsula. Moreover (though William could hardly have known this) he indulged in furtive political intrigue, aimed at discrediting Wellington's conduct of the campaign.

No. 26.

Falques,
Febry 7th 1813.

My dear Father,

Yours of the 9th of Jany I received some few days since and was very sorry to hear that Jack had met with so serious an accident, which, as you observe, has been attended with every fortunate circumstance that could alleviate so distressing a calamity and I trust the most tedious and helpless part of his confinement is already over. He will probably recover sooner than an older or more weighty Man but I do believe the Doctor's first Sentence is six weeks Bed. His getting over the Lane Hedge with a broken Leg is almost incredible and exceeds every Exertion I ever heard of, although wounded Men in the Field of Battle when strongly operated on by fear, discover Powers which are nearly equal to it. I commend his Defence against Mrs Stevens amazingly and trust the Lady is now aware that very few Stomachs are strong enough to digest such stale Rations.[1]

About this Time I received your last Letter, I myself met with a Piece of Ill luck, which upon service is only second to Bodily Injury. I allude to the Loss of my best Horse by the Glanders, for which the Mare I bought of Heywood was shot on the 30th of January, and I assure you her Loss is to me almost irreparable as very few Horses are now equal to my Weight which has encreased beyond conception since my arrival in this country and I now dread getting into the Scales. This Mare was only five Years Old, had no appearance of Disease when I bought her and was every thing I could possibly wish for, but I suppose the very severe Bevouacs at the close of the campaign brought on this fatal Disorder, which is very prevalent amongst the Troop Horses, tho' as you well know it is unavoidable and cannot by any precautions be guarded against where the Horses have been so continually exposed. I do not wish to conceal from you that I was improvident enough to give 100£ for her. One half of this sum I shall recover almost immediately, and as the Mare cost Heywood nothing, he may if he chooses considerably lessen my Loss without any inconvenience to himself; but this I have no right to expect.

I am exceedingly obliged to you for your offer to Purchase a Troop, for which I am eligible in May next, should one be vacant, but I rather imagine our zealous Captains will quit Service before the Campaign commences, in which case the Troops will be sold out of the Regiment. By a reference to the 'General Regulations for the Army' (which every Officer ought to have), you will find the regulated Difference is 1785£ and when you see another Captain gazetted, would be obliged to you to notify to the Agents your readiness to purchase for me, and I believe you should say the Money is in your Bankers' hands. I have at present no wish to change my Regiment, although the brilliant Accounts of Count Platoff's Cossacs [during the Retreat from Moscow] almost make me waver.

The 23£ in Stephenson's Hands I have given to Mr Dry, whose demand appears to be a just one, tho' I cannot conceive why he never reminded me of it in England. He says he delivered his Bill when I paid another, which I suppose was the case as I had not the least Idea of such an account. I have at present a better kit than I ever had before in consequence of having taken the whole of a diseased Officer's clothes who was the largest Man in the Regiment, notwithstanding which his Things fit me very well.

I have this Morning been gratified with an account of the Russian successes, in comparison with which the Battle of Salamanca dwindles into a daily Skirmish. I wish to God I had been with the Russians as nothing can equal the Delight of pursueing an Army, especially a French one, and I am happy to see that the French attribute all their Mischief to that contemptable little Island. 350,000 more Men to counteract the Intrigues of England, delight me beyond Measure, and I hope now we have got him down we shall kick him about. Lord Charles [Manners] has received a political Letter which does not intimate an Idea of Peace but says Bounaparte has recovered his Health and is indefatigable in his Exertions to recruit his Army for another Campaign. The affairs of Spain continue pretty much in statu quo with an abundance of success on the part of the Guerillas, which, *when true,* is always confirmed by Lord Wellington, who very seldom has an opportunity of garnishing his dispatches with any brilliant Success on the part of the potent Allies.

I was very sorry to see Lord Wellington's Letter to his Generals commanding Brigades and Divisions [of 28th Nov.] at full length in the rascally London Newspapers with suitable remarks by the Editors, one of whom cooly observes the Army was in a state of Mutiny and the Retreat more dreadful than that of the French through Russia. My own opinion is that Lord Wellington never wished or intended the aforesaid Letter to be published, nor was it, I believe, in many instances read to the Troops but to the Officers only. It was perhaps rather too violent and never would have been necessary had his Lordship proper General Officers under him or Men of his own choosing. At present the Ministers or Duke of York order out a batch of Generals, who in general have neither Talent or Experience. Some blunder is committed, Lord Wellington speaks his mind, the Great Man is offended or probably sulky at being crossed, and never bothers to exert himself or act upon his own Judgement again. Here I think commences a slackness which is quickly felt throughout the whole Machine, occasions incalculable Mischief and has induced Lord Wellington to call this 'God Almighty's Army' a thousand times.[2]

Except General Hill there is scarcely a General Officer in this

Army of any Talent and very few of any Activity except Sir S. Cotton and I suppose no commander ever had so few clever Men on his Staff almost all of them being coxcomical or Old Women, amongst the latter I include Col. Gordon, the Quartermaster General, who—I believe—has returned to England after doing considerable Mischief instead of saving several Millions a Year, for which purpose he was sent out.[3]

I have been expecting to move from hence several Days in consequence of our want of Forage. The Reg^t is extremely sickly and I believe I might say the same of the Army.[4] I have written a sort of a Chronicle which would amuse Jack during his Confinement as it is very different from any one that was ever written before.

I cannot hear any news of the Parcel you sent Cartwright, tho' I have yet a Box to receive from him containing Clothes and I hope it will be found within a great Quantity of the Men's Necessaries [which] have been ruined by being kept so long in damp Store Houses.

Have you killed any Woodcocks this Year? In this Country I have not seen one and in England I never found so many as we frequently did last Winter near Castelo Branco.

I beg you will give my Love to Mother, Sister and Brother and Believe me, Your dutiful Son, WILLIAM BRAGGE.

P.S. Whenever we have a Peace, I propose taking a Trip to the North in order to see Petersburg and all the Russian Generals, who certainly have some pretty Names.

I was glad to hear of Jack being free from Pain. When Major Clowes broke his Leg, he never suffer'd any and I hope Jack will be equally fortunate. Are you not nearly as badly off for Horses as I am?

As William had expected, the Regiment had to move on again four days later, this time to Souré, near the mouth of the Mondego river where it remained until 19 April, Easter Monday.

William next wrote towards the end of March. Wellington recently had been created Duque da Victoria by the Portuguese. Gen. Cartwright was the Colonel of the 3rd Dragoons. Lord Cathcart was the British Ambassador at the court of St. Petersburg. Sir Robert Wilson was the military correspondent at the Allied headquarters in northern Europe.

No. 27.

Souré,
24th March 1813.

My Dear Father,

Two or Three English Mails have at length arrived at the same Hour, by which I received your letters of the First of Feby and Third March (an intermediate one arrived some weeks before) and I am happy to find they all give so favourable an Account of [the Progress which] my Brother Jack is making towards soundness and I trust he will hereafter feel no Inconvenience from an Accident of so serious a Nature.

Your Letters were delivered to me whilst sitting on the Town Bridge and had your Friend the Major been alongside me he would in all probability have gone over the Parapet and into the purling Stream for contradicting you at Frampton, as what I before stated was the real fact. The Affair of Col. Hervey and his Orderly took place at another Time and positively on another Road from that on which Sir E. Paget was taken. The Col^l had been dining with the Division left as the Rear Guard and returning in the Dark accidently rode up to the Enemy's Vidette who was a German. The Officer of the Picquet was at that Moment visiting his outposts with a few Followers and some conversation about his (the Col.) deserting took place between them before the Col^l perceived his Mistake. He immediately made his Escape but the Orderly's Bridle was seized and the man made Prisoner. This Account Col. Hervey gave Sir S. Cotton. I should add that the 14th are brigaded with the Germans and that the Colonel speaks the Language.

We hear nothing of the speedy movement of the Troops but probably our Information and the Route will arrive by the same Post. Should we be allowed Three Weeks more, the Cavalry will in every Respect be more effective than they were last Year and much better appointed. Our Brigade will muster upwards of Fifty File a Squadron, which for Service is very strong, although the establishment is 85 Horses a Troop. The last General Orders relate to the 11th and 9th Light Dragoons and 4th Dragoon Guards giving up their remaining Horses to other Regiments and marching themselves to Lisbon for immediate Embarkation. I cannot say I should like for the Third Dragoons to be of the same Party, for the Ninth and Fourth Dragoon Guards have suffered themselves to become perfectly ineffective without ever having lost a single Man or Horse in Action. The 11th are a most excellent Regiment and are reduced to a state of Inefficiency by the Loss of a whole Squadron soon after their Arrival and by having been repeatedly opposed to a great superiority of Numbers, particularly in the late Retreat to Valladolid, and I believe no Men ever behaved more gallantly than they have done on every Occasion.[5]

It is rather unfortunate that I did not enter the Regiment Three Months sooner, as Heywood's Troop is now for Sale and I shall become a Stepping Post for a Junior Officer; but I rather expect it will go out of the Regiment all together, which is the best thing that can happen for me as the Duke may otherwise say that Promotion in this Regiment is going on too rapidly. In the Event of another Troop's being [available] before May, I shall prevail on Lord Charles to ask Gen¹ Cartwright to keep it open for me, which he will most likely do without Difficulty. What an Escape I had in not going into the Greys where I should still have been a Cornet!

Ever since I lost Heywood's Mare, the Cream Colour has been Dog lame or I should have had no difficulty in selling her. I shall still wait and see if she gets round and then, as you advise, give her and some money to buy another. She is at present in beautiful Condition. Was I anywhere near the Eleventh, I could easily get mounted at this moment [for] I suppose they will scarcely take Horses to England. You had better not trouble yourself about sending me a Horse as it is attended with some risk and a good deal of Trouble. The Colonel could not well allow a remount Troop Horse to be given to an Officer, as a Dealer sends out two or Three Lots of Officers' Horses every Year which are taken to the HeadQuarters of the Cavalry, valued by a Board of Officers and disposed of by Lot.

I understand our Staff Corps and Artificers are constructing Buildings on the Agueda to be used as Hospitals in case of another Advance into Spain as the Rascally French have literally destroyed Salamanca and all the Colleges and Convents which we used for that purpose.[6] The Infantry are to have Three Tents per Company and the Officers of Cavalry one each—a Regulation which will probably save the Lives of Thousands of the former.

We dined together last Sunday for the first Time since our arrival in Portugal and contrived to have a sumptuous Dinner consisting of all the Delicacies of the Season, a Sirloin and round of Beef, a roasting Pig and Kid roasted whole, which had the appearance of a large Dog. I dined another Day with a Portuguese Gentleman, who—barring Oil and Garlick—gave us a capital Feast not much unlike 'the Dinner after the Manner of the Ancients'. I can eat Oil in Soup but do not *yet* much relish Garlick or Horse flesh.

Cox writes me word that Mrs Farquarson is received into all the best—or rather highest—Society in Dorsetshire and has been at Parnham, where I understand Sir W. [Oglander] means to vegetate for the remainder of his Life and keep less Company every Year. I remember Portman or some other Candidates calling Dorsetshire a *Proud County* which was certainly misapplying the Term unless it means cringing to riches.

The Spanish Nation are more sanguine than ever in their Expectations that the French will evacuate the Country this Summer. The Enemy are certainly exacting their contributions with more rigour than ever, are more anxious to get Money than Grain and continue sending everything towards Valladolid and Burgos, which looks as if they intended taking up a defensive Position either on the Douro or Ebro. Caffarelli and Soult are certainly gone to France and I sincerely hope the latter will not return, as he is beyond Doubt one of the First Generals in the French Army and better able to cope with his Lordship than any other.[7] What a Distance we have to march to come up with the Enemy. The Hussars and Life Guards have yet farther, as the former are still at Lisbon (under Col. Grant) and the latter at Santarem and Tomar.[8]

We are extremely anxious to see the next Newspapers which will probably contain Dispatches from Lord Cathcart and give us the Debate on Lord Wellesley's motion.[9] Your Account of Sir Robert Wilson is, I have no doubt, correct as he did something of the same sort with Lord Wellington who I know disliked him very much.

With kind Love to my Mother, Brothers and Sister, Believe me Your Dutiful Son, WILLIAM BRAGGE.

P.S. Madrid Gazette March 10th:

18 Generals, 56,000 Infantry and 7,000 Cavalry at Madrid, Toledo and Segovia. I fear they do not intend running without some hard knocks.

Since early February, Wellington had been planning his next offensive. He was emboldened by Napoleon's debâcle in Russia, news of which had recently reached him. No longer would he need to content himself with containing the French Armies in the Peninsula. By taking full advantage of the British naval supremacy of the coasts in planning a combined strategic move, there was a good prospect of ridding Spain of the French altogether.

Although Wellington told his brother at Cadiz that he hoped to start out on 1st May, he gave no hint of his intentions. In fact the first definite information of his objectives was given in a letter to Beresford on 24 April. The Secretary of State for War was not told anything until 12 May, the day on which the offensive began. It is particularly interesting therefore that William, writing also on 24 April, should have to a large degree correctly forecast Wellington's intentions for his father—nearly three weeks in advance of the official dispatch to England.

During the winter there had been several changes in the command and dispositions of the French Armies of the North, Portugal, Centre and South. They were now commanded by Clausel, Reille, Drouet and Gazan respectively. Gen. Sir John Murray now commanded the Allied force at Alicante.

No. 28.

Pinheiro,
24 April 1813.

My Dear Father,

Our Festivities for the Year 1813 commenced on that auspicious Day stiled, by the Aldermen of London and other good Xtians, Easter Monday, on which Day we arrived at the celebrated Seat of Portuguese Learning and have since continued our Route on the Direct Road for Oporto, where we shall probably cross the Douro in the course of a few Days. We have known for some Time that it was his Lordship's intention to move us in this Direction but had no Idea that our Plan of Operations for the ensuing Campaign was really to commence at so early a Season or at so great a Distance from the Enemy, whose Line of Defence will probably be turned by this very Manoeuvre, as it is well known from an Intercepted Dispatch of Soult's that the Douro at Valladolid was to protect his Right Flank and the Guadarrama Mountains beyond Avila his Left Flank, leaving the River Adaja in his Front which runs completely across from Left to Right. This, from the Dispatch of Soult to the Minister of War, was to have been their Line of

Defence[10] but if Lord Wellington marches his Cavalry by Braga and Braganza entering Spain in considerable Force in that Direction (which already appears pretty evident), we shall probably act in conjunction with the Galician Army and compel them to fall back towards Burgos. Our Brigade, the Light Dragoons and Heavy Germans are between Coimbra and Oporto and we have beyond it some heavy Columns of Portuguese Infantry.

We have hitherto found the Roads extremely Bad and have marched long Stages but the country improves at every Step and I cannot possibly conceive anything more Delightful than this immediate Neighbourhood, which affords a fine Prospect of Aveiro Bay and a distant view of the Sea. The Vines instead of being allowed to run along the Ground like Gooseberry Bushes are either supported by Trellace Work or trained up in Trees which has a very pretty Effect. Corn of every Description is in abundance and I am just fattening a Troop on Green Barley now in Ear. What would Old Fowler say to see me and my Reapers in our 6 Acres! !

I have contrived to get myself well clothed during the Winter and start with an English Cheese, 6 Pounds of Tea and 16 of Gold Dust. My Cavalry I have not yet arranged but have supplied the Place of the Mare with a Spanish Black Stallion which I bought at Heywood's Sale for 100 Dollars, being one Half of what he gave for it. He is better than Fourteen Hands high and has a fine sweeping Tail but I do not intend that the French should see me on him. The Spanish Horses are nice little Hacks, very safe, easy and hardy and according to their Accounts swifter than the North Wind. The Cream Colour is lame and I shall change her for a Mule immediately. The Portuguese at Souré offered me 100 Dollars for her to go in a Carriage over the Stones at Lisbon.

I have written to one of our Men at Lisbon who I think would answer you extremely well as Bailiff if his Friends do not provide better for him. I consider him a good Scholar and, from all I can gather, believe him to be of unexceptionable Character for Honesty. He is a man of extreme good Connections and quarrelled with his Friends by going for a Dragoon in which Capacity he was shot through the Thigh at the Glorious Battle of Salamanca and was *on Crutches* when I last saw him. I now understand he is discharged at Lisbon, from whence he will probably write to me in the course of a few Days. He is rather more than Thirty Years of Age and has a Wife without Children who bears as good a Character as her Husband.

The latest News we have in the Portuguese Newspapers is the confirmation of Lord Wellington's Title of Duke of Victoria and should this 'Man of many Names' be fortunate enough to bring the French to another General Action, I trust we shall again have good Reason for another Pension and Title. King Joseph still remains in Valladolid, the Army of Portugal at Palencia and that of the South at Madrid, whilst Suchet and Genl Murray are too near Neighbours to remain long without some serious Dispute.[11]

I am glad to hear that Genl Cartwright recommends me to succeed Heywood, although I had not the most Distant Idea of being allowed to Purchase, in consequence of not having served 3 Years. But I since have written to the Commanding Officer and have had that Letter forwarded to the General with such a supporter that I do not conceive he will allow any exchange or any Promotion in the Regiment to my Disadvantage. Should I be fortunate enough to obtain a Troop early in the Summer, there is every Hope of my having two Juniors before Xmas.

What a lucky fellow Jack is to escape so often, but I hope he never will attempt leaping Carts as well as Stiles as few People have ever escaped for a second leap. I am not very angry at my Severe Sentence from the Dorchester Assizes and really think I should have deserved a more severe Punishment for keeping a serious Countenance during that delightful Evening at Sydling.

When well bit with Fleas at some miserable Hovel in the North of Spain, I shall think of my present Quarters where I have a suit of Apartments, a good Stable, excellent Bed and am myself the largest Man in the Village, although my Patron is Lord Lieutenant of the County. And if my Eyes and Nose do not deceive me, there is a ------ in the Garden—mirabile dictu.

25th April.
Our Route is arrived. We cross the Douro at Oporto on Thursday the 29th and march into Cantonments in the immediate Neighbourhood of the City of Braga, famed for making the Warmest Shawls in the World. I am delighted with the Idea of

seeing Oporto and marching by a new Route into Spain. I start with 6 pounds of Tea, an English Cheese, Keg of Brandy and 4 Doubloons beyond my Pay.

With Love to my Mother, Sister and Brothers, Believe me my dear Father, Your Dutiful Son, WILLIAM BRAGGE.

P.S. If the Dragoon I mention will undertake the Situation and is not a *cripple for life,* I am confident he would be an honest Servant and a great Acquisition to you but his Friends are so well able to provide for him and would find him so useful in a mercantile Office, that I fear I shall not succeed in getting him for you.

You will be vexed to hear that I never received the Telescope and Map, although the Method I pointed out to you is the regular and safest Mode of Conveyance as a Serg^t is appointed at Lisbon to take charge of and forward Officers' Parcels which arrive by the Packet.

By early May, Wellington's intentions of a mighty outflanking movement were becoming apparent to the whole Army. On 12 May the cavalry brigades and infantry regiments began to march out to various assembly points. This was twelve days later than intended because the delayed spring had provided inadequate forage during April and the vital pontoon train for the Douro and the Esla had taken longer than expected in making the overland journey from Vila Velha.

The 3rd Dragoons, with the rest of Ponsonby's heavy brigade, reached Braganza on 22 May. William wrote the following day, happy to tell his father of the immediate prospects for the Army and that at long last the map and telescope had reached him.

The Sadborow Yeomanry was a detachment of Dorset militia, raised from the estate and commanded by William's father.

No. 29.   Braganza,
                                            23rd May 1813.
My Dear Father,

As I think it may be many Weeks ere I shall again have Time or Opportunity to write to you, I shall send you a short Epistle from the Northern Extremity of Portugal giving you as much Information as I can collect of the present Situation and future Destination of our glorious Army, which is now on the point

of commencing active operations against the Infernal Pack of
Bounaparte, whose Hounds will, I expect, be well whipt in this
Season, by Prince Kutusoff and Lord Wellington.

Our Brigade arrived yesterday in as good order as could be
expected after having crossed the Province of Tras os Montes
by a Route never before attempted by British Cavalry and which
never ought to have been marched. We were two Hours getting
up one Hill, and for three Days never got the Regiment out of
single Files, scrambling over Rocks, Mountains, and Precipices
for 8 Hours every Day. We halt here Tomorrow and on the 25th
move on towards Benavente, near which place we shall arrive on
the 30th; we have with us the 1st, 3rd, 5th and 6th Divisions of
Infantry and two Portuguese Brigades—about 2,000 each—a
Brigade of Guns with each Division, and a Troop of Horse Artillery attached to the Cavalry, which consists of our Brigade, the
Heavy Germans, the 12th and 16th Dragoons and Seven Squadrons of Portuguese Cavalry. The whole of this Force is under
General Graham[12] and is to advance on this Side of the Douro
whilst Lord Wellington is advancing by Salamanca with the remainder of the Army and is probably at that City this Day,[13]
therefore your Newspapers will now become more Interesting
every Day, and I trust their Columns will be garnished by another splendid Victory before the 1st of July.

The French have divided their Force, and do not appear to be
aware of this deep laid Scheme but have had their Eyes solely
turned on Lord Wellington, who has remained at Frenêda col-
lecting a large Force and deceiving the Enemy, who will probably
cross the Douro in double quick Time as soon as they know of
our Column being on their Flank. They have Troops at Salamanca, Toro, Zamora, Valladolid and Benavente and have established Posts on the Esla, but the current Opinion is that they
will immediately Fall Back towards Dueñas and Burgos and
should they *not feel* themselves equal to a General Action on
that Ground they must retire across the Ebro.

Their Force is estimated at only *55,000* Infantry and *10,000*
Cavalry at HeadQuarters, but I cannot believe they are so weak.
If it is so they certainly will not meet us but if (as I suppose),
they have *80,000*,[14] with a King at their Head and Lots of Generals, who consider French Troops invincible and have never had
the Honour of contending with the British General, a General

XII. The Victory of Vitoria.

From an aquatint in the collection of Col. Crookshank.

XIII The Battle of the Pyrenees, 28 July 1813

Action will be adventured and I am sanguine enough to expect as Brilliant a Victory as we gained the last Year on the Plains of Salamanca, which would oblige the Enemy to evacuate the other Quarter of Spain. Few People, however, are so sanguine in the Expectations as I am, which I am sorry for, as a croaking Officer dispirits the Men.

I expect a Letter from you shortly deploring the Loss of a Telescope and Map accompanied by a *Threat* never to trust any thing more (which has to go through so many Hands) on the Briny Ocean; but I now have the Happiness to assure you that the Directions I gave were the best and the most certain, and that the aforesaid Glass and Map arrived safely and were delivered to me on the 20th of May about 4 Leagues from Braganza but could not have left England before April, as immediately on its arrival at Lisbon, it was put on Board a Transport and forwarded to Oporto and from thence brought on the Commissariate Mules without Loss of Time. I had so completely given up all Hopes of these necessary Articles for a Campaign, that I had been at the expense of procuring others of an Inferior Quality. I have now to thank you for the Trouble you have taken and to assure you that the Glass is—in my opinion—the best in the Army, and when drawn out at full length and placed on a Wheel Barrow, would have the double effect of perceiving the Enemy and deterring them from attacking a Post defended by Light Artillery.[15]

The Twelfth Dragoons have this Morning past through the Town in a Dress like anything but a British Soldier and I think it would be advisable for Lord Wellington to make his Cavalry, in their new Dresses, rank off before the Infantry, or Hundreds more will be shot by their Friends this year than *were* last. The Hussars and Life Guards are with Lord Wellington, therefore we have not had an opportunity of seeing them. The Men have all Helmets, *Saches* and *Sabre* Taches, the two latter being considered of more importance than a Curry comb and Brush.[16] Our Brigade is considerably more than 1,000 strong, which is very well, although not above two Thirds of what they originally embarked from England.[17]

I told you we were not pleased with Lord Wellington at the beginning of the Winter and that I thought he would find himself not so popular in the Army. He has now given the Infantry

H

Tents and our Brigade *350 Guineas* for Horses and Guns taken at Salamanca, besides *1500* Dollars for the Horses taken at Llerena in April 1812, therefore he is again a fine Fellow and our Colonel a great Blockhead for not allowing his Men a Drunk: it could but last three Days at farthest, as Wine is three Halfpence a Pint.

If I take more than Two Eagles, the Sadborow Yeomanry shall have a Standard, and if King Joe falls in my Way, my Mother may depend on a very Beautiful Diamond Broach which I understand is to be found in his Neck Cloth.

I like my Stallion very much and have been offered a decent English Mare for him. He is very safe and honestly worth 50£.

They say the French have Ten Thousand Cavalry, but their best Troops have been withdrawn—that is the Polish Lancers, Imperial Guards and Gens d'Armes.[18]

Be kind enough to give my Love to my Mother, Brothers and Sister and believe me Your Dutiful Son, WILLIAM BRAGGE.

P.S. Trusted to a Portuguese Post Office.

Graham's left wing crossed the Spanish border on 26 May and once over the Esla, pushed rapidly eastwards. Wellington rode off from Salamanca to join his second-in-command on the 29th, leaving Hill with his corps of 30,000 to advance to the Douro, and within a week the whole of the Allied army of 81,000 was concentrated north of the river near Toro. The first French line of defence had been turned with scarcely a shot fired.

From there, by using a powerful cavalry screen to prevent the French from observing his movements and by marching rapidly across the broad, corn-growing Tierra de Campos well to the north of their positions, Wellington turned all further attempts at resistance. The lines on the Carrion, the Pisuerga and the Ebro itself crumbled like that on the Douro. On 21 June, the greater part of the Allied army closed in on the French armies of the South, Centre and Portugal (the last at half strength only because of an ill-timed loan of three divisions to Clausel) in the small valley before the town of Vitoria. By nightfall French pretentions to the domination of Spain had ceased to exist.

William described the Battle of Vitoria, the effects of which were even more decisive than those of Salamanca, and the lightning march across the north of Spain in a letter written three days after the French had been put to flight.

No. 30.

Ordian, a Village on the Road
from Vitoria to Pamplona,
7 leagues from the latter.
June 24th 1813.

My Dear Father,

Having been once fortunate enough to give you the earliest Confirmation of a most brilliant Victory, I could not refrain from making a second Attempt, and for that Purpose prepared a very Laconic Epistle on the Field of Battle; but as the Mail did not go off so speedily as I expected, and as I no longer possess any chance of Introducing this Letter into Lord Wellington's private Bag, I shall endeavour to give you a more detailed Account of our Glorious Victory, in which greater skill on the Part of our General and greater Bravery on the side of the Troops was more conspicuously displayed than at the Battle of Salamanca, and I trust greater and more permanent Advantages will result to the common Cause of Europe from the most brilliant and decided Victory.

On the Morning of the 21st we found the Enemies Army (supposed to be 70,000 Men)[19] strongly posted in rear of the River Zadorra and about 3 Leagues in front of Vitoria, their Left Flank resting on and defended by Mountains [the heights of Puebla] apparently inaccessable, a River and two immense Woods in their Front and their Right Flank defended by the same River, the Banks of which were on their side most favourable and capable of Defence. The greater Part of our Army were in the Plain in Front of the Enemy's Position, which appeared so strong and was so well planted with Cannon that I had no Idea we should attempt to force it. In this state of Affairs with a partial Cannonade Lord Wellington appeared to threaten the Woods in their center, but we soon perceived one Division under Genl Hill clambering up the Mountains and threatening the Enemy on their Left, whilst our Brigade was sent round to their [own] Left, where we found that Genl Picton with the 3rd Division had crossed the River and gained Possession of the high ground [the knoll of Ariñez] on the Enemy's Right Flank, Genl Graham having likewise passed the River still more to their Right and towards their Rear. From this moment Victory seemed to lean on our Side. The Enemy fell back, however, in admirable order, taking advantage of the numerous Villages,

Woods and Inclosures, and keeping up a tremendous Cannonade on our Troops who continued advancing, successively driving them from Wood to Wood until they reached Vitoria, from whence they were still forced and driven a League beyond, being four Leagues from when the Battle commenced; but the Ground was so intersected with Woods and Inclosures that the Cavalry could not act against their Infantry, and their Cavalry took care to keep out of the Way, which accounts for our not having taken more Prisoners. The Battle lasted until Night stopt our eager Pursuers, and for the last Hour the Horse Artillery were serving them with Grape and Cannister Shot at 80 and 100 Yards distance, so you may suppose their killed and wounded were pretty numerous, tho' they seldom waited for a Charge of Bayonets or many Volleys of Musquetry.

Our Loss is heavy and probably amounts to 2,000 in killed and Wounded, amongst whom are few Field Officers and no General, whereas the French to our Knowledge lost 3 General Officers on the Field of Battle, and the Bridge [at Gamarra Mayor] where Graham crossed was so crowded with Dead that it was necessary to remove the Bodies to allow our Artillery to pass.[20]

Our Trophies consist of upwards of 120 Guns, all their Ammunition, all their Military Chest, all King Joseph's Coaches and Baggage—in one word *Wheel Carriages*—to the amount of *2,000* (without my getting any Plunder), Mules and Horses *1,000* and about 1,500 Prisoners besides Lots of Stores of every Description.[21]

As I said before, our Cavalry had little to do during the Day except support the Infantry, which we did the whole Day and once Wheeled into Line to charge the Cavalry but upon seeing us advance, they dashed into a Wood and escaped.

The Secresy and Rapidity of Lord Wellington's movements will probably astonish Europe as much as it has the French who have been completely taken by surprise, having found our Advance where they expected Guerillas only and our main Army where they expected our Advance. The Weather and Roads have been sadly against us and the Army has been and still is short of *Bread* and the Cavalry without *Corn*, which, added to extreme cold and Tempestuous Weather, has greatly thinned the Ranks of the latter.[22]

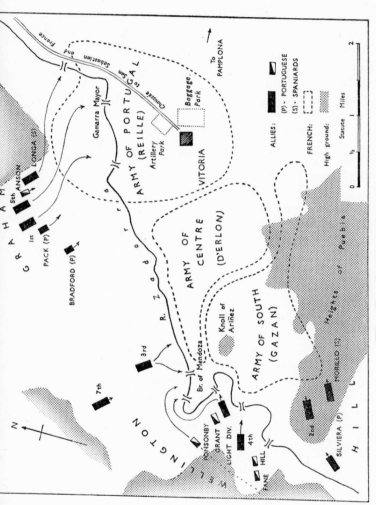

III. The Battle of Vitoria

We left Braganza on the 25th May and arrived at Tabara on the 28th, crossed the Esla by a Bridge of Pontoons on the 31st, Palencia 7th and in sight of Burgos on the 12th. On the 15th [we] crossed the Ebro by Puente Arenas, on the 18th our Light Division surprised their Light [at San Millan, a hamlet 40 miles west of Vitoria] and took nearly 400 Prisoners and all their Baggage, and on the 21st we entered Vitoria. We are now within 7 Leagues of Pamplona with the French Army in a Quandary as his Lordship is making some Misterious CounterMarches, [so] you may shortly expect to hear of a Division of their Army being cut off or of some great Advantage being obtained.

I may as well add that I had a View of the whole Battle from Morning to Night and have been fortunate enough to bring off a proper Proportion of Legs and Arms.

We have only halted one Day since I wrote to you from Braganza and were then reviewed by Lord Wellington, the whole Brigade averaging 48 File a Squadron.

Accounts differ relative to the Force of the Enemy and many persist in it that Suchet was in the Field with 14,000 of his Army, others that he was there but without any of his Troops and many believe he was not near the place.[23] The King was seen and chaced by Lord Worcester and 10th Men and only escaped by the Breadth of a Mill Pond.[24]

But for the Intervention of Lord Wellington on the 12th Inst., the 3rd Dragoons would have been well beat on the very ground where they were severely cannonaded in our former Advance on Burgos.[25]

With kind Love to my Mother, Brothers and Sisters, Believe me, Your Dutiful Son, WILLIAM BRAGGE.

[On Cover: LISBON JY 18 1813]

The broken French armies from Vitoria straggled back to Pamplona, where a strong garrison with eighty guns was left, and beyond to France. Meanwhile those forces which had not been engaged in the Battle were receiving Wellington's attention. Graham was pushing the northern remnants under Foy towards the Bidassoa, and in the upper Ebro valley Clausel with his Army of the North was also being hard pressed. Ponsonby's brigade, together with Grant's Hussars, supported four divisions in a movement southwards from

Pamplona, which was designed to intercept Clausel as he tried to extricate himself. The Army of the North, however, managed to slip past to momentary safety at Saragossa.

William wrote from Tafalla on 1 July, after the pursuit had been called off.

Sir Stapleton Cotton rejoined the Army at the end of June. He had been on sick leave because of his Salamanca wound since December 1812. Champneys, William's youngest brother, was about to take his matriculation.

No. 31.

Tafalla,

July 1st 1813.

My Dear Father,

I have this Instant been informed that Letters for England must be sent to the Office in Five Minutes, therefore I fear you will as usual have a very dear Half Crown's Worth; but we are so constantly on the move and in Camps, that I will not lose even this opportunity of acknowledging the Receipt of your Letter of the 2nd April which arrived this Morning and also of giving you a hasty sketch of our Adventures since the 21st, which have not been quite so fortunate as we had every reason to expect.

The French Army retired during the Night of the 21st as far as Salvatierra, perfectly disorganised, and from Daylight on the 22nd until they reached Pamplona were never out of Fire of our advanced Guards. They had with them only 2 *Pieces* of Artillery and one Howitzer and one of these was taken before they reached Pamplona, where they left a Garrison and retired across the Pyrenees. One Division under Clausel arrived within Two Leagues of Vitoria (from Logroño) on the 22nd before they heard of the Fate of their Army[26] and were immediately pursued by the Sixth Division with Mina's Cohort checking them in Front. They retired to Tudela and were coming on towards Pamplona when an infamous Alcaldy (Magistrate) in their Interest, informed the French General of our marching to intercept him, which, but for this Information we certainly should have done Yesterday or the Day before and made our complement of Prisoners which I am sure John Bull wants.[27]

A variety of Papers of consequence, Maps, Plans etc., were found in the Carriages of the King and his Suite and amongst

others a confidential Letter from my Imperial Brother requesting that the Army should be withdrawn across the Pyrennean
Mountains, bringing with it all the Artillery and the Heavy
Guns from Madrid and Burgos and upon no consideration to
allow them to fall into the Enemies Hands. What will he say for
himself?

We crossed the River Aragon and returned to this Town
yesterday, where we hope for a few Days Halt as our Work has
lately been extremely Harrassing. Sir S. Cotton has not yet arrived but his Staff expect him here Daily. The Hussar Brigade
are at Olite about 3 Miles off and are to be broken up immediately and brigaded with more experienced Regiments, being
found to be perfectly unacquainted with their Duty as Hussars
and having nearly Galloped their Horses to Death. They are
very conceited and extremely Jealous of our Brigade which
has been working with them and is at present Twice as
effective.[28]

Sir Thomas Graham has been threatening France with Invasion and pursued the French as far as Tolosa, where several
sharp Skirmishes took place [on 24th–26th June] and in which
both Spaniards and Portuguese preceeded the British Troops
and fought admirably. The old veteran was slightly wounded
but I believe is still in the Field with his Troops. He is about 66
Years of Age and beats all his Aides de Camp by dint of hard
Riding.

I have seen Pamplona through the Glass at about Half a Mile
distance. It appears to be a regular Fortification, pretty strong
and I should suppose difficult of access from being in a Plain.
Our Troops have broken Ground before it, but the Heavy Guns
cannot arrive before the 9th or 10th of this Month in consequence
of Bad Roads. We have the old Story of a Garrison composed of
Invalids, of want of Provisions and other Idle Stories but I fear
it will cost us Two Thousand Men if it stands a Siege. They have
a Reg^t of Dragoons and about 3,000 Men within the Walls,
which are too extensive for the Garrison.

We are in a delightful Town surrounded by Miles of Garden
Ground abounding with Fruit and Vegetables and within it an
Inn, Billiard Table and Tennis Court.

I am glad you have once more visited the Metropolis and seen
the New Theatres, young Lions and Lionesses, which from

your Account do not appear to have much improved in the space of Twenty Years. I should very much like to rig myself out with every Convenience for this Campaign but am for two Reasons glad you did not spend any Money on my account, as in the first place I do not expect another Campaign in this Country, and if there is one, I shall probably not see it as a Troop would send me Home immediately. One of our Majors is going to get a Lieut. Colonelcy and one of the Capts. to sell out, in order to avoid coming on Service where the Duty of a Captain is comparatively nothing. [Genl] Cartwright promises that no Capt. shall exchange, therefore I hope few weeks will elapse ere I shall be Gazetted. If you wish to send me anything by a Remount, address a Line to our Regimental QuarterMaster, Mr Brunton, who is a good Man and worth more than all the Officers at the Depôt.

I am glad to hear you have placed Champ under a good Tutor at St Mary Hall and sincerely hope he may not disappoint us.

Col. Grant's Brigade Major is James Croft of the 15th; if you ever saw the Parties you will not think the *Black Giant* and *Red Dwarf* bad names.

I must now conclude with making many apologies for this Hasty Scrawl, and with kind love to my Mother, Brothers and Sisters, subscribe myself Your Dutiful Son.

WILLIAM BRAGGE.

[On Cover: LISBON AU 25 1813]

Wellington spent the next three weeks consolidating his position on the Bidassoa river and astride the mountain passes into France, and preparing for the sieges of San Sebastian and Pamplona. During this time there was little for the cavalry to do. The 3rd Dragoons remained at Tafalla until mid-July and then moved to Larraga, 10 miles to the west, when forage became scarce.

On 20 July William heard that he had received his Troop and had been gazetted Captain. Two days later, on the anniversary of the Battle of Salamanca, he wrote to his father telling him the glad news.

O'Donnell, a Spaniard of Irish extraction, commanded the Reserve Army of Andalusia, which had followed up the bulk of Wellington's forces.

No. 32.

Larraga,
22nd July 1813.

My Dear Father,

I have two days since received the gratifying Intelligence of my having been Gazetted to a Troop in the Third Dragoons and shall consequently lose no Time in returning you my sincere Thanks for your generous Exertions on my behalf, by which you have secured me a rapidity of Promotion almost unprecedented and placed me on an equal Footing with Officers who have been Ten Years in the Service and made every exertion to accelerate their Promotion.

I have hitherto expected that the Official Notification of my having been promoted would be accompanied with an order to join the Depôt at Canterbury, which I am sorry to say will not be immediately the case, as the Man who gets the Majority was on the effective Strength of the Troops abroad and will by returning to England only leave the proper Complement of Capts in this Country. Therefore I must remain until regularly relieved, which may not take place for Two or Three Months, although Lord Charles has lost no Time in ordering out some of our Shufflers in England, who must now either show their Faces in this Country or retire, and as I know few of them have any Inclination for Service, I have sanguine hopes of being out of the Break within Two Months from the Period of being Gazetted.

I never recollect being so Tantalised with reports of Letters and Newspapers as we have been lately in consequence of Two Mails having arrived at HeadQuarters without bringing any Letters for the rest of the Army, which are probably gone round by Lisbon. Our latest Papers are of the 16th of *June* and Lord Wellington's up to the Third of *July*, so you may suppose we are not a little anxious for the Daily Arrival of the Orderly, and I do firmly believe the Mail must arrive this Day about Two Hours after this Letter goes to the Post.

I can tell you no sort of News respecting the Army nor shall we know one Tittle of what has taken place since the Battle of the 21st until the London Newspapers arrive; Clausel has retired from Saragossa [into France] by way of *Jaca,* where he has left his [six] Guns in possession of Genl Paris, who commands Suchet's advanced Guard and [who] was Three Days since at the latter Place with 5 or 6,000 Men. Suchet [is] at the former with the remainder of his Army, having succeeded in relieving all the Garrisions except Pamplona and St Sebastian. He will now probably retire unmolested but I believe Lord Wellington has possession of all the Coach roads, therefore their Artillery must be destroyed and left behind.[29]

I *believe*, we have given up Pamplona to O'Donnell's Army of about 22,000 Men whilst our Troops are busily employed at St Sebastian, which certainly will be speedily taken; but as for the former, I have too good an opinion of the French to suppose that Spaniards will ever get them out of a strong Fortification except by Famine, and I have no doubt that the Enemy are tolerably well provided against so potent a Foe.[30]

I understand that our Troops on the French Frontier are regularly soaked with Rain every Day and half Frozen at Night, which I can easily believe, as even we perceive a sensible Difference in the Climate here and in Old Castile and Leon. We could last Year scarcely support the Heat, whereas I am now writing so good and steady a hand in consequence of having lately (at Noon) left off playing Fives in the Church Yard for two Hours.

What I hinted before respecting our Hussar Brigade has already taken place in part. The 18th are sent to the Germans to learn Out Post Duty and the 10th and 15th brigaded together [with the recently arrived 7th] under Lord E. Somerset of the 4th Dragoons, whilst the Black Giant has been under the Necessity of retiring to England in high wrath. It was understood that the Prince had sent Grant out to this Country with a Promise of Commanding the Hussar Brigade and every one considers that Lord Wellington has acted well, in not chusing to allow such an arrangement.

We have about 600 Dragoons and nearly 1,000 Horses expected Daily at Bilbao, a Reinforcement which will render our Cavalry more effective than ever, and as only two Regts are employed at this Moment, I think our Force will astonish the French if we cross the Frontier. Besides the Portuguese and English, Lord Wellington has collected a very powerful Spanish Army, all well armed, cloathed and equipt, and I very much doubt whether they have had so good and powerful a Body acting conjointly for this last Century as at this Moment.

Our Mail has arrived and brought with it an old Newspaper for me and a Letter from Champ, who concludes his Letter by informing me that you are very ill and Jack looking very ill, which I am extremely sorry to hear, but as the young Man is not likely to observe his Degrees of comparison, I trust his Account was at that Time an exaggeration and that at any Rate you have ere this recovered from your Indisposition, a piece of Intelligence I should gladly have received from you by the same Post. . . .

I hope sincerely that amongst other Advantages arising from my Promotion, I shall have an opportunity of paying you a visit ere long, for tho' I am certain you will rapidly believe that I had sooner run the Risk of a Campaign in this Country than be a constant attendant at Drill in England, nevertheless I should be delighted with a few Months leave of Absence, which, besides giving me an opportunity of seeing my Friends, would also enable me to add considerably to my comfort by purchasing some of those little conveniences you saw in London, the Necessity or superfluity of which I know so well how to appreciate.

We are on the River Arga, 3 Leagues from Tafalla. Sir S. Cotton gives a Dinner to the Brigade in commemoration of our glorious Struggle this Day Twelve Months.

With Love to my Mother and Sister and sincerely hoping I may shortly find you all in a State of Health and Happiness, I remain my dear Father, Your dutiful Son,

WILLIAM BRAGGE.

[On Cover: LISBON SE 3 1813]

Napoleon heard the news of Vitoria at Dresden on 1 July. After recovering from his wrath and indignation, he sent Soult, who had been spending two idle months at his headquarters, to salvage the situation on the Pyrenees at the earliest possible moment.

Joseph had realised that his days were numbered but he felt it the greatest insult that he should have to accept the very man who earlier had been such a thorn in his side as his successor.

Soult reached the Army on 11 July, assumed command the following day and immediately set about re-organising the forces at his disposal. Within a fortnight he launched a powerful offensive through the Maya and Roncesvalles passes to relieve Pamplona.

Wellington was caught unawares, having believed San Sebastian to be more important to the French. Inadequate information from the Passes and inept appreciation by the local commanders in his absence allowed the French Marshal to push as far as Sorauren, less than five miles from Pamplona, before Wellington (riding swiftly to the scene) was able first to stem the attack and then beat the French back to the frontier.

The 3rd Dragoons with most other regiments in the rear were called out at short notice when the danger was realised. When William next wrote, Soult had been bundled back to the border, badly mauled and demoralized.

No. 33.

Barrastain,
3rd August 1813.

My Dear Father,

As often as the French serve us out a plentiful Ration of Shot and Shell, I shall consider it my Duty to acquaint you that I have not received a greater Allowance than I can easily digest without any Assistance from the Doctors, and indeed were it not for this Consideration, I should scarcely venture to give you the slightest Information of a Series of the brilliant Affairs which have led to another decided Victory and once more overwhelmed a French Marshal and his Army with Shame and Confusion. . . .

Nothing could be more unexpected than the Order we received on the Evening of the 26th to march on the following Morning at Three O' Clock for Pamplona, in the neighbourhood of which we arrived at Noon and to our utmost Astonishment received Intelligence that our Troops had been forced back from Ronces-valles and were to retreat the following Morning towards Vitoria, with our Brigade covering their Guns (pretty Prospect).[31] In the mean Time Arthur arrived with considerable Confidence, tho' exposed to a Tremendous Tempest. . . .[32] We kept march-ing until Ten at Night.

During that Evening (27th), we could plainly perceive that Pamplona was illuminated and I since understand that the Gates were opened and a superb Entertainment provided for Soult and his Staff, who unfortunately was detained that Even-ing by a Prior Engagement. The next Morning (28th) he had turned our Left Flank and his Troops were pushing down a Valley to relieve their Friends when the Head of our 6th Division coming in Sight occasioned a slight Interlude and the French were forced to retire under *Three Fires*.[33] After this they four Times endeavoured to carry our Left and were four Times re-pulsed at the very point of the Bayonet. Then Center and Right

[were] attempted, but whether opposed to Spaniards, Portuguese or English, they met with the same Fate and were constantly repulsed with immense Slaughter, although great Numerical Superiority and fresh Troops were constantly opposed to the Allied Army.

On the 29th they buried their Dead, and on the 30th they retired after making two more desperate Efforts to gain our Heights and when I last saw the Gentlemen, both their Flanks were turned and our own Men in immediate pursuit. Our Loss is great, their's enormous, and I have no Hesitation in Asserting that this little Excursion has cost the Prince Regent of Spain 20,000 Men without effecting any one single Thing except a comparative small loss of killed and wounded on our Side.[34]

Nothing but a Man, a Mule or Goat can Travel up the Field of Battle, therefore the Cavalry on both sides were kept completely in the Back Ground and our Infantry alone entitled to their hard earned Laurels. We still remain in a miserable Village near the Position and about one League from Pamplona, which is still rather watched than Blockaded, as the Garrison are making Daily Excursions and reaping all the Wheat round the Walls. It appears to be a most delightful City and regularly Fortified.

We have not yet received Newspapers with an account of the Battle of Vitoria in consequence of the Post going round by Lisbon, but I understand John Bull was delighted, and as he usually judges of the brilliancy of the Victory by our List of killed and wounded, he will be still more gratified with the last Action, as our Loss is greater than at Vitoria.

We hear that King Joseph and Jourdan were not kindly received at Paris and that the command of the Army was immediately given to Soult with the Title of Prince Regent of Spain.[35] Upon his arrival at the Army, he assured them that he would commence offensive Operations in eight Days, relieve Pamplona on the 27th, and once more cover the French Arms with Glory; and as the Army had greater Confidence in him than any other General, their Expectations were great at the first Attack. Afterwards, Blows, Example of the Officers and Threats of the Martial were in vain. The Troops would not advance nor do I think they ever will against our Army, which will recruit faster than theirs and be more effective in a Month's Time than at present.

Yours of the 28th of June I received about a Week since and am happy to find you do not give so alarming an Account of your Health as Champ did, altho' Thoroughgo Nimbles are bad enough in all conscience. I am extremely sorry to hear of Cox's misfortune and do not think Mrs Egerton attributes it to the right cause. By the bye, how is the Pontifex and what does he think of the War—that we are going to the Dogs head foremost? For my part I expect to hear that Pamplona and St Sebastian have fallen and as we once more possess the Passes, I do not see why Lord Wellington should not ration 100,000 Men in France for a Month or Two—an attempt of the sort would, I think, hasten a Peace.

We have 200 wounded Frenchmen in every Village for Miles. A Flag of Truce went into Pamplona Yesterday for medical Assistance and 3 Surgeons were immediately sent out.

Lord Charles says I must be relieved before I can go home but I confidently expect an order to join the Depôt in a few Weeks.

With Love to all, believe me, Your Dutiful Son,

WILLIAM BRAGGE.

After the two Battles of Sorauren had been fought and the famished remnants of the French had stumbled back to the safety of the Bidassoa and the Passes, the French garrisons settled down to the defence of San Sebastian and Pamplona and the Allies to the reduction of them.

The 3rd Dragoons remained close to Pamplona for the first week in August and then moved to quarters at Decastillo, from where William wrote his next letter towards the end of the month.

Lord Aberdeen was about to leave for Vienna to persuade the Austrian Emperor to re-enter the War.

No. 34. Decastillo,
25th August 1813.

My Dear Father,

Yours of July 26th and Lucy's Letter of a much earlier Date only arrived last Night in consequence of the Packets having been sent round to Lisbon, but as we had previously received Newspapers up to the Fourth of August, I trust we never more shall have occasion to send Letters so far to the Rear.

We remained in the Neighbourhood of Pamplona about a Week after the Battle and nearly dished all our Horses by keeping them so long on Wheat. We then marched into our present Quarters about 2 Leagues from Estella, where we hear, and know, much less of what has taken place in the Pyrenean Mountains than you do, who are so much farther from the Scene of Action. We hear that Lord Wellington has recommenced the Bombardment of St Sebastian,[36] a Place which from its peculiar situation appears to be very Difficult of Access, but whenever the Town is in our Possession, I understand the Castle cannot possibly contain the Garrison longer than is necessary to settle the Terms of the Capitulation. Pamplona has been most wretchedly invested ever since the British left it, the Garrison not only taking possession of the Guns of the Spaniards but, I understand, a Cavalry Picquet has been taken and all the Wheat round the Town reaped and carried into the Citadel, notwithstanding which, the Odds at head Quarters are as high as Ten to one that Pamplona falls before St Sebastian. Don Carlos de España invests the former; he is known to be a Rogue, and I firmly believe will one Day or other prove himself a worse Character.[37] Whenever the Gates of Pamplona are open, I shall go and see it as it appears to be a most beautiful City.

I believe I rated Soult's Loss at 20,000 *Men* in my last Letter, which I now understand was considerably under the Mark.[38] It appears from all Quarters that there never was an Army so beat before and Lord Wellington in their Retreat continued to be with them every Morning with a Fresh Division before Soult had left his Camp. They were never allowed to march on the Roads and were driven off the highest Mountains by a handful of Men, in short the Valour of the British and Portuguese Troops at the present Moment exceeds all credibility etc. I trust Lord Wellington will allow about *100,000* to draw their Rations in France before the Winter comes on, just to retaliate for their Conduct in Spain and Portugal.

They say Lord Wellington's Reinforcements from England and Portugal have now arrived, which will enable him to maintain his Position against any Force until the Garrisons in his Rear surrender.[39] Before the 20th, Soult was in Motion and I understand occasioned some alarm.[40]

Navarre is a most delightful Province and I really believe,

XIV. San Sebastian during the siege.

From an aquatint in the collection of Col. Crookshank.

XV. View of Bayonne from the sandhills.

altho' the smallest, certainly the most Loyal and Patriotic in Spain. Their great Leader is Mina, who is a wonderful Man. About 3 Years since, his Nephew was taken and killed by the French, upon which occasion this Man (who was then a Farmer) adopted his Nephew's Name, took the Command of a Battalion which he had raised and by a continual succession of bold, skilful and daring enterprises has worsted the French 24,000 *Men*, encreased his own Force to a Legion of Ten or Twelve Thousand who are all Volunteers and the best organised Troops in Spain, well paid, fed and clothed. . . . [He is] now a Major General and Governor of the Province, the whole of which has the greatest Confidence in him and to a Man sing the Praises of Mina and Lord Wellington. They say Mina is very merciful and never kills the Prisoners unless they are badly wounded. The Garrison of Saragossa marched past here and the Officers said four Men had been shot that Morning.[41] They consult the Surgeon if a Prisoner knocks up, who at once passes Sentence as we do on a Glandered Horse.

Amidst the Pleasures of Navarre, I have two or Three Miseries to complain of. In the first Place you cannot ride out of the Village without being absolutely covered with the Showers of falling Chaff; secondly you can't sleep after Daylight, eat or drink without swallowing a Legion of Flies, and Thirdly, every chair, Bed, Brick and Tile swarms with Bugs, who although they do not bite me, occasion a great deal of Trouble, for as T. Spencer said of worse Varmint: 'They look so scandalous about ones *Clothes*.' The Produce of the Harvest is immense and is all brought in on Crook Horses as in Devonshire.

Our New Major is returned to the Depôt, with positive orders to send out a Relief of Capts but as our Heroes in that Quarter seem to consider this Country 'The Bourne from whence no Traveller returns', I fear it will be some Time ere I shall see you. As it is, I understand one Captain has bolted, which is the Thing of all others I wish for. Should opportunity offer, I shall certainly pay a vizit to the Pyrenean Mountains, which we hear is the most Beautiful Country in the World for those who admire the Picturesque.

I long for another Packet as I look upon it [to] our sending Lord Aberdeen to the Congress [which] would assuredly lead to a Peace, tho' I hope we shall drive the French out of this Country

I

first. I do not think the Spaniards reinforce Lord Wellington so fast as they ought to do, nor do I think the Junta and Cortes remaining at Cadiz a likely Measure to give the People Confidence. The Spanish Armies distress the Country for Rations more than the French. O'Donnell's Army is not more than 11,000 and they demand Rations for 20,000, one Reason which makes our Cause unpopular.

I hope your Account of Major Frome is not altogether correct. Some of his earliest Measures in India occasioned a *Mutiny* in his Reg^t. One of our Officers knew him there and I will learn the particulars of his Death. Estella is a capital Town, but what is a Town without English Manufacture? If Applin could Land in the Square with his Stock in Trade, he might have his Price and depart with the Dollars before Sunset. Only conceive a City where you cannot purchase a Cup and Saucer. I have dined with Thoyts once and intend to pay him a Vizit at Logroño, which is the best Town on the Ebro. . . .

We are still Paid in Guineas, which pass here for 23s. 6d.

What Champ says of me at Vitoria I deserve. I was amidst all the Carriages the next Morning and *made nothing.* [There were] Lots of Ladies' Jewels [and] Lace Dresses, some of which you will probably see round *Mrs Grant* at Weymouth, as I hear the Col^l was active.[42]

We had some capital Races Yesterday and I won everything I ran for. I have a Poney which beats every thing of her Inches.

With kind Love to my Mother, Brothers and Sisters, Believe me, Your dutiful Son, WILLIAM BRAGGE.

P.S.

I should have thought a Spanish Wife would have been as well received at Sadborow as a Spanish Horse, but you shall be gratified as he won me *two Races* Yesterday. He beat some English Horses and runs again on Friday.

CHAPTER FIVE

Into France

September 1813–April 1814

After the fall of San Sebastian on the last day of August (and Pamplona two months later), Wellington's operations were determined largely by those of the Northern Allies. When definite information had been received that Russia, Prussia and Austria were all once more moving against Napoleon, he forced the line of the Bidassoa and a month later, in early October, crossed the Nivelle. The Allied success at Leipzig encouraged him to push across the Nive and threaten Bayonne in mid-December. For the next month bleak, wet, wintry conditions prevented further activity, for, as Wellington was at pains to point out to the Secretary of State for War: '. . . In military operations there are some things which can not be done; one of them is to move troops in this country during or immediately after a violent fall of rain. . . . Our operations must be slow: but they shall not be discontinued.'[1]

Meanwhile the 3rd Dragoons, together with the other heavy cavalry regiments, had remained well to the south in Navarre for the broken country of the Pyrenean foothills was no place for large forces of cavalry. After a long period at Decastillo, the Regiment had marched shortly after Christmas to the scattered villages close to the east of Vitoria.

Between September and the New Year two of William's letters never reached his father. Whether this was due to being lost at sea in the particularly violent gales of that winter or due to being intercepted at sea by one of the few maurauding French or American frigates will never be known. William was aware that his letters had gone astray when he next wrote in January 1814.

Lord Castlereagh, the Foreign Secretary, had left England for the Allied Headquarters in Germany in mid-December to preserve the unity of the Allies, baulk any unilateral peace offer to Napoleon and safeguard the British stipulations for a permanent settlement.

No. 35.

Eguileta,
Jany 12th 1814.

My Dear Father,

I did not receive your Letter of the 16th Decbr before Saturday last and shall therefore lose no Time in answering it, as I am almost convinced you have lost one or Two of my Letters. I shall also take this opportunity or requesting you to direct your Letters to *Spain,* as I sometimes lose a fortnight by their going round by Lisbon.

We have since Saturday received another Packet bringing Newspapers up to the 30th [December] which have nearly frightened me out of my Wits with rumours of Peace, but as the *Courier* usually writes the Sentiments of the Ministry, I hope with the Editor we are not going to be juggled into a fallacious Peace but that Lord Castlereagh is gone to the Continent to entreat the Allies to prosecute the Contest until a complete Balance of Power is established, which now apparently requires only a little more Exertion to be completely accomplished. This Wish probably appears in *me* more selfish than Patriotic at this Instant as a Peace under Existing circumstances would undoubtedly send me to the Plough-Share; but I trust by a little threatening and Manoeuvring to gain another Step in the Regiment as we have one Capt who is kind enough to indulge his good Natured Brother-in-Law with campaigning in his Place, and would allow him to remain here for ever if we do not interfere, and as exchanging Duties is not allowable amongst Privates, it still less ought to be suffer'd amongst Officers.

I mentioned the circumstances of my having sent some Lace and a Shawl Home by Genl Ponsonby's Aid de Camp in a former Letter, but as it appears you never received it, I shall now acquaint you that my reason for not writing a Note at the same Time was that my Friend was mounted and waiting in the Street [in] which I was making the Purchase. I am glad to hear from Lucy that Mrs B. was pleased with the Shawl. As for the Lace, it was not what I supposed it, but can it be very dear at 4d per Yard?

As you sound anxious to hear about I. Phelps of the 28th Regt, I wrote to his Adjutant to enquire what had become of him and received the answer I expected: 'That the Man alluded to in my Letter was *severely wounded* in the Arm on the 13th In^st [December, the Battle of St. Pierre, close to Bayonne] and gone to the Rear.'[2] The Adjutant himself probably does not know in what Hospital he is in, and if he did, it would be out of my Power to render him any Assistance, as it is against the Law to advance Men Money in Hospital.

We left our old Quarters in Navarre two Days after Christmas and are now cantoned in miserable Villages between Alegria and Vitoria, eleven of which with difficulty contain our Regiment, being nearly two Parishes to a Troop. I have one Half of my Troop in this dirty Hole consisting of 12 Houses and the other half are two Miles off. We are in a Valley between two Ridges of Mountains which are covered with Snow and the Roads are so deep and Muddy that we have little or no communication one with another. These Comforts [are] considerably heightened by the coldest and most Tempestuous Weather I almost ever experienced, which makes me wish myself out of the Country fifty Times a Day. The Road from hence to Vitoria is the same the French went after their Defeat and is *now* completely strewed with paper and old Rags. The Guns are still formed up near Vitoria and although many have been removed, it is still the finest and most extensive Park of Artillery I ever beheld.

Lucy is very Misterious about Susan Adney and says she is greatly mortified at her Conduct and almost fears she may *yet do worse,* which I think by no means improbable as I am confident her Husband is a poor, weak jealous Creature and not by any means likely to keep so lively a Lady in order. Her ci-devant Lover, Capt Hamlyn, is at Vitoria, but as he behaved very improperly to Lucy at Exeter, I shall not be at the Trouble of calling on him. The Hussar Brigade are in France and very much dejected at seeing their Horses exposed to a hard Service at this Time of the Year without Hay or Straw and very little Corn. One Brigade of Cavalry and Artillery together with one half of the Waggon Train have been starved there already. Sir S. Cotton has got a pretty considerable command in the Front with Genl Picton under his orders, therefore you may expect to hear of more Bloodshed shortly; one fights for spite, the other for a Title, and I believe Genl Paris is to be the Victim.[3]

We have heard from our Depôt as late as the 25th, at which Time the remount had not marched and probably never will, unless Lord Castlereagh can rouse the Allies to another Fight. Our brave allies the Spaniards are such undisciplined Vagabonds that Lord Wellington has been obliged to order them to the Rear, in order to defend the French Peasantry from Depradation.[4] You may rely on it that no two Nations are more opposite in every particular than the Spaniards and English and no two Armies can detest each other more. We hope to see one Rascal Sus: per Col: for the most cowardly and villainous Murder of the Honble Capt Gore of the 94th, who was shot in his Passage by order of a Spaniard, who together with his armed Crew were driven out of the House into the Street by the said Capt and his Servant *in their Shirts*.

I am glad to hear that the Heavenly Sir rides so well hunting but fear he will have much longer runs of a Sunday if he does not give up doing Duty gratis, especially whilst such modest Men as Festing are in the Neighbourhood.

Being quite alone and without any Prospect of Company in this Village, I have commenced reading Hudibras for the first Time of my Life, which of course necessarily renders my Evenings bearable. I occasionally correspond with two *Spanish* Parsons, and have besides one in the House who understands my Lingo pretty well, but I have at present unfortunately lent an English Parson my Dictionary, which of course curtails my conversation.

If I had not written this badly, I should have told you with a better Face that Lord Charles considers me a 'very legible Scribe'.

With kindest Love to my Mother and all the Family, Your affectionate Son, WILLIAM BRAGGE.

When William next wrote at the beginning of February, little change visibly had taken place in the positions of the opposing armies, but Wellington, heartened by the news that the Northern Allies had crossed the Rhine, was preparing a new offensive. At the same time Soult was discomfited by Napoleon's summary removal of three of his ten divisions.

Down near Vitoria, though, there was little to disturb the 3rd Dragoons in their widely scattered village quarters.

No. 36.   I have not yet received Cap^ts Pay *8 months* due.
Eguileta,
Feb^ry 8th 1814.

My Dear Father,

I am sorry to find that the Family were so long in a state of anxiety in consequence of not receiving any Letter from me, a circumstance I can only attribute to the ill Fate of some unfortunate Letter which has been thrown overboard in order to escape from the hands of the Enemy, as I am not aware of having neglected you so long as your Letter of the 8th Ult^mo mentions, nor shall I forget to give you the earliest Information of the probability of my Return.

We have this Day received Letters and Newspapers of the 27th [January] and by one of the former we are informed that our Remount left Canterbury on the 15th, together with one Capt and some Subalterns which were to embark immediately on their arrival at Portsmouth. Two Cap^ts were ordered but upon one of them producing a sick certificate, the next turn Boy has not been ordered in his place, in consequence—I presume—of the commandants being on the Brink of Marriage with his Sister-in-Law. It is a shabby Business, by which I am again in a state of uncertainty as it depends upon Lord Charles whether he will permit me, or an Officer who has been Gazetted since me, to return to England on the arrival of this Remount. His Lordship is now with Head Quarters, therefore I cannot yet discover his Intentions, tho' I have reason to suppose he will decide in my Favour. In the mean Time I have made ample Provision for another campaign by purchasing new accoutrements, repairing all Breaches, strengthening my necessaries, reinforcing my Stockings and shoeing my Boots with all dispatch. . . . There is no knowing how soon we may be called upon, as the Light Dragoons cannot at this Moment raise a Trot whilst we are in the highest Condition, and as our Adjutant clearly proves, with 70 Horses less, are 27 stronger than we were this Time Twelve month, and nearly the same with regard to the Men, as we then had upwards of 100 Sick and have not Ten at present.[5]

Lord Wellington is much against Officers transferring their Menageries from this country to England, therefore if you add me the Bay Mare to your collection of Living curiosities, we shall be extremely fortunate. The large, Handsome Mules of this country are only fit for Draught or Burthen and the little ones—tho' more active—are in my humble opinion as Tumble down Devils as any Gentleman would wish to ride upon. The Asses are generally weaker than in England but not so stubborn and the large ones almost as rare as in England. The famed Merino Sheep would Disgrace a Gentleman's Flock [6] and in short neither Men, Women, Horses, Dogs, Asses or Mules are worth importing into England, and I hope never to see any thing Spanish there but a Prisoner, a Dollar or a Bolero Dance.

Wednesday 9th Feby.

You will probably not be much surprised to hear that Capt Oglander passed through Vitoria a few Days since on his road to join his Regiment. I have not the Pleasure of knowing him but had I been half so unlucky as he has been, I should certainly have cried out: "Hold, enough". Lord Charles writes us word that he has bet 200 Gns. that there is a Peace or Buonaparte dethroned within these Two Months, which is—I suppose—the general Opinion at Head Quarters.[7] Everything is in readiness to pass the Adour as soon as the Roads and Weather will permit, but hitherto any Military Movement has been impracticable from a Deluge of Rain which has rendered the Roads impassable. Mules cannot travel more than a League a Day and the Roads fairly strew'd with Carcases of Horses, Bullocks and Mules. The cavalry have not averaged more than 4 lbs of Corn per Day and are without any Forage but Furze. In St Juan de Luz the Inhabitants are making a good Penny of the English but in all the Villages the French are much distressed and, of course, wish us at the Devil. If we want to gain a Party in France, I presume Lord Wellington cannot do worse than advance the Spanish Troops, as they cannot be restrained and from the Archbishop of Toledo to the Dirty Volunteer are bent on the Lex Talio—in short they have so long robbed their own Countrymen, that they cannot be expected to spare their Enemies.

I suppose I told you before that my Village consisted of Twelve Houses and that I had no Company but myself. My Misery has been still farther encreased by Twelve Days Snow, therefore to relieve myself from ennui I sent for a *Young Man's Book of Knowledge* and boldly attacked a Position defended by Multiplication and Division. The Enemy made a most obstinate Defence and I believe we were fighting *3 Nights* with various success before the Enemy yielded to Perseverence and Obstinacy; the loss was nearly equal on both sides but amounted to many Millions. I believe I may say with young Sturt that I have been so long learning Division that I have forgot my Multiplication.

I must allow that the Spaniards are good Gun Makers and as the Factory is but a few Leagues from hence, I intend bringing Home a Specimen. They are cheap, very light and short in the But. The Shawl I intended as a Xmas Box to the Patrona, and the Trimming for my Two Sisters. I think the Shawls so handsome, that I shall bring Home as many as I can afford. I must take this Letter 3 Miles to the Post Office and then start two Leagues in the contrary Direction to purchase a Map of France at Vitoria.

With kind Love to my Mother, Brothers and Sister, Believe me, Your affectionate Son, WILLIAM BRAGGE.

On 12 February Wellington launched his attack, which was designed to split Soult's force and drive the greater part inland away from Bayonne. Within a fortnight the French Marshal had been thrown back to the Gave d'Oloron, some 25 miles from Bayonne, and the isolated town had been invested by Sir John Hope with 18,000 British and Portuguese and 12,000 Spaniards. Sealing off the town had been severely hampered by a particularly violent storm which had raged for over a week. As one observer put it: 'old Ocean did not approve . . .'[8] of the plan to build a bridge of boats across the Adour just inside the bar of the river mouth. Yet in high winds, rough seas and in confined, treacherous waters the difficult naval operation was carried out successfully with few delays.

Further south in Spain the Winter Quarters were bustling with activity. On 25 February Ponsonby's brigade was ordered out and together with other cavalry brigades began the march up the Grand Chausée from Vitoria to St. Jean de Luz, where the 3rd Dragoons arrived on 4 March.

William wrote the same day.

No. 37.   St Jean de Luz,
                                                    March 4th 1814.

My Dear Father,

You perceive by the date of this Letter that our Brigade has at length infringed upon the sacred Territory by crossing the

Bidassoa with upwards of 1,000 Horses in the finest condition imaginable and I sincerely Hope with that Advantage on our side, a few Weeks will elapse ere we shall again have an opportunity of showing ourselves worthy to participate with our brave Infantry [in winning] those Bright Laurels which they alone have been entitled to for this last Year and half; but tho' I talk so ambitiously, it will appear from this Letter that I prefer gathering those Laurels alone which are found in a certain Path near Sadborow, which although not the direct Road to Honour, is a line more sought after and more conclusive to the ease and convenience of his Majesty's Subjects than the troublesome Path of Ambition. Joking apart, our Remount has landed and I and Capt. Branfill will in a few Days receive an order to join the Depôt at Canterbury, which we purpose taking Advantage of the first fair Wind and tranquil Sea, but at present the Weather is so tempestuous and this Shore so dangerous, that were I to get Lord Wellington's leave Tomorrow, I should not venture on Board until the Weather became more settled. We arrived here Yesterday—Time enough to see Eleven Vessels wrecked in the Harbour and many others have been lost at Sea. Such Wind, Rain and Thunder as we have had for these few Days past I never before remember and to Night it still continues pouring.

The Brigade halts Tomorrow but will probably cross the Adour the next Day. As for News, I cannot venture a Word for Lyes are so current that we do not know who to believe, but every Body agrees that the French (although fighting with unusual obstinacy) have hitherto been most decidedly licked. No one knows where Lord Wellington is, the nature of his Wound[9] or what he is going to do, but I conceive as Six *new* Eighteen Pounders passed through here this Morning, Bayonne will be attacked immediately. The French have *10,000* Men and will probably make a cruel Defence, especially if the Garrison are all like 160 Prisoners I saw Yesterday—all stout, able and well looking Men.[10]

I want to see Bayonne, to sell four Horses, get some Pay, return to Passages and find out the Day before I embark, therefore a fortnight will elapse before I make a start but I will write you word when and on what Ship I go on Board. I intend bringing Home my Mare but shall most likely trust my own Carcass in a Packet as she can generally either fight or run away.

Our Brigade is fortunately not Quartered in the Town or we should have lost half of the Men from Intoxication as the Vessels wrecked were full of Brandy, Rum and Beer. Two of our Men *are dead* and many more Dead drunk. I believe amongst Soldiers and Sailors 15 lost their lives from Drinking last Night.

St Jean de Luz is a very nice Town and the Women really Beautiful and not the least like Spaniards or English. The Town is quite full of English Shops but chiefly for the accommodation of the Army, and I do not think many of the original Inhabitants are here, tho' they have probably fled to more dangerous Quarters. They speak French, Spanish and Basque here but the latter (a Language only known to themselves and the Biscayans) is more generally spoken. I know nothing of French but am a pretty good Spaniard, that is to say, I could pass through the Country without an Interpreter, as I understand them and with little Difficulty can make myself understood. You say right that Priests ought to understand Latin, although not one in 500 knows a Tittle of it.

The Road from hence to Vitoria is most delightful and winds you round the Mountains without passing over any and the People are, I suppose, the best Agriculturalists in Spain. They cultivate Cider and dig the Land instead of Ploughing it—the whole Country is strewn with his Majesty's lean Kine and unless the Army get better Meat than what I saw on the Road, they will certainly Die (like the Cows) of the Starve—it is really shocking.

If I get Money enough, I mean to smuggle a few things, but as for Liquors, the only good Wine and Brandy comes from England. I suppose I shall be thought *poco Valiente* for leaving the Regiment at the commencement of another Campaign, but if I did not go home, some one else must and those who have seen a Campaign know there is nothing in it particularly inviting—I mean that People *like Browne* of Frampton would insinuate I had run away.

I must leave one of the turn-downs for the News of Tomorrow Morning and shall conclude for the present by desiring my kindest Love to my Mother, Brothers and Sister, begging you to accept the same from your dutiful Son,

WILLIAM BRAGGE.

Sunday 6th I believe.

Fremantle passed through here last Night with Dispatches from Lord Wellington, therefore you will know all the News before this arrives—the Remount joins us to Day but I shall cross the Adour Tomorrow with the Regt. We are to be under Sir John Hope [Genl Graham's successor] and cover the Siege of Bayonne. The Country is so deep and intersected with Ditches to that Degree that Cavalry cannot act.

Ponsonby's brigade, temporarily commanded by Lord Charles Manners, marched over the bridge of boats below Bayonne and then on inland through Peyrehorade to join Wellington, who was continuing his encircling movements to pin Soult against the Pyrenees. The Regiment reached Aire on 14 March and was present at Soult's delaying action close to Tarbes on the 20th.

William was released to return to the Depôt at Canterbury on 12 March but he stayed with the Regiment until it reached the vicinity of Castlenau-Magnoac on the 22nd, at which time the French were falling back rapidly on Toulouse.

William's last letter from Spain was written from Passages while he was waiting eagerly for his ship to sail for England. Meanwhile a hundred and fifty miles away Wellington was looking for a suitable place over the Garonne above or below Toulouse before delivering his final blow of the Peninsular campaign.

No. 38.   Harbour of Passages,
                                                  3rd of April 1814.

My Dear Father,

Inclination rather than Necessity induced me to remain with my Regiment longer than I intended when I last had the Pleasure of writing to you or I might at this Moment have been some Weeks in England, but I prefer'd marching 150 Miles through the most delightful Country I ever saw, and after having once more escaped from a sharp Fire [at Tarbes], have made good my Retreat to the Sea and embark'd my self and my Mare on Board of the *Fanny* Transport, No 98, and shall probably arrive in England about the Time you receive this Letter, unless our Commandant thinks proper to wait for contrary Winds and Tempestuous Weather. For some Days past we have had the most favourable Winds and I concluded that a Fleet which sailed from hence on the 31st has already made the happy Land.

I left the Army on the 22nd and arrived here on the 31st without encountering so many Difficulties as I expected, as our Party was small and almost totally unacquainted with the French Language, our Route discretionary and the whole Road thronged with formidable Banditties, who are encreasing fast in Numbers and have already made considerable Depredations on our stores and Convoys. In consequence of this latter circumstance, we were compelled to march back by the same circuitous Route we took in marching up, or we might have arrived at Passages 3 Days sooner and sailed with the last Convoy. As it is, we shall probably move the Day after Tomorrow.

I have on Board with me 3 Officers of the Guards who appear very good natured, Gentlemanly Men and take longer in cleaning their Teeth than I do dressing myself entirely; but as we are likely to agree and have made a Bargain with our Master to furnish a most excellent Table for 50 Dollars, I have no doubt of a very pleasant Voyage. Two Officers of our Brigade who came down the Country with me, delayed on the way at St Jean de Luz and consequently could not be on Board the same Vessel which I rather regret.

I sold the cream coloured Mare and Old Brown Horse (both foundered) at a considerable Loss, but the sale of a Poney and Spanish Horse have brought me upright again. A Man gave me 30£ for the Mare upon condition that I should get a Passage for his Portuguese Brute for a Col. of the Cork Militia now at Plymouth, which I have accordingly done and have the animal safe on Board. The most Hazardous thing I ever adventured was bringing the Two Horses in an open Boat through 500 Sail of Shipping and over or under twice as many Ropes and Cables, but we got them safe on Board without meeting with any accident.[11]

We are bound for Plymouth and Portsmouth but I shall of course land at the former if possible.

I left Ld Wellington about 20 Leagues from Toulouse, where I suppose his Lordship is at present, as it was supposed he would be very well received there. Every Day he halts, he will be joined by 300 British Infantry besides which, the Household Brigade—1,400 strong in capital condition—the Portuguese Cavalry, several Remounts, 6 eighteen Pounders, 500 Spaniards and 2,000 Portuguese are following in succession, and—I believe—some

Thousand Spanish Cavalry, therefore his Army must accumulate Daily whilst Soult's Army is diminishing by continual Desertion. The Siege of Bayonne is finally determined on and the 7th Division [is] marching from Bordeaux [which threw its gates open to Beresford on 12th March] to assist the 1st and 5th Divisions. I think the Works are very strong and that we shall lose 5,000 Men before it falls.[12] I saw St Sebastian Yesterday but not any feature of its former Beauty now remains, the whole Town being a heap of Ruins.[13]

As we are likely to meet soon, I shall not trouble you with more at present but beg you to give my Love to my Mother, Brothers and Sisters and accept the same from your dutiful Son,

WILLIAM BRAGGE.

P.S.

I am going to make a little Fortune by exchanging Guineas for Dollars and Bank Notes.

Five days later—two days before the Battle of Toulouse—William sailed for England. He arrived at Plymouth on 16 April and was greeted with the wonderful news of Napoleon's abdication and the end of the War. What better homecoming could there have been!

The following day he wrote to his father telling him of the safe return of himself and his little bay mare.

No. 39.　　　　　　　　　　　　　　　　Plymouth Dock,
　　　　　　　　　　　　　　　　　　　April 17th 1814.

My Dear Father,

I have great Pleasure in informing you and my Mother of my safe arrival in England after a Short but very rough Passage. I landed my own precious Carcase Yesterday and Two Horses to day, one of which is not my own. I shall start my Man with the Mare Tomorrow Morning for Sadborow and follow myself in a Day or Two, but I wish to stay with Lucy and Adney (whom I have only seen for Minutes) to see whether they are bound for Ireland or not.

My Helmet is so novel a sight in Plymouth that I absolutely cannot wear it without being mobb'd, and in order to escape Mr Polito's Cage, have purchased a round Hat and Plain Suit of Clothes—Dock made—and was forced to remain in Bed until

Mʳ Levi the Jew had furnished me with a clean Shirt and Stockings.

I left Passages on Good Friday, at which Time the glorious and very desirable conclusion to this terrible War was not known, and when our Army hear of it, I think all except Lord Wellington will be Mad and certainly Drunk for Joy.

I have scarcely Time to conclude this Letter, therefore you must excuse haste and believe me, with Love to all, your dutiful and most particularly happy Son, W. BRAGGE.

3. KING'S OWN DRAGOONS.

XVI. An officer of the Third (King's Own) Dragoons *c.*1814.
From a contemporary pen and wash sketch.

XVII. The Little Bay Mare.

Epilogue

Although William may have regretted leaving his Regiment just before the closing stages at Toulouse, he in fact returned to England only three months ahead of it. The 3rd Dragoons played only a minor part in the battle for the city and afterwards remained encamped in its vicinity until the 1st June. The Regiment then marched across France and landed at Dover on 20 July, almost three years to the very day after sailing for the Peninsula.

For the next year the Regiment was stationed in the Midlands and in the North of England. When Napoleon's attempted grand coup had culminated in his crushing defeat at Waterloo and H.M.S. *Bellerophon* lay waiting at Rochefort, the Regiment embarked as part of the Army of Occupation of France. The 3rd Dragoons, with William among them, reached Paris on 19 August, where nearly eight weeks later, they were present for the Grand Review of the whole of the Allied armies by the Emperor of Russia, the King of Prussia and the Duke of Wellington.

The Regiment served in France until November 1818, first at Nantes and then for the greater part of the time in the Pas de Calais. On its return to England, it was converted to a regiment of Light Dragoons and sent almost immediately to Ireland. During this service William was appointed a J.P. in County Limerick.

William's later years followed a conventional pattern. He married in 1824 and was gazetted Major on half pay in June 1826. He then spent several years on the Continent caring for his wife during a prolonged illness and ultimately inherited Sadborow in 1843. For the rest of his life he devoted himself to the well-being of the Parish of Thorncombe (where his brother Jack was the Vicar), to the care of his estate and to his growing family of eight children with all the quiet, generous attention of a benevolent, unassuming country gentleman. In 1853 he finally retired from the army (having risen to Colonel on the retired list) and in that year he was also appointed High Sheriff of Dorset. He died at Sadborow on 6 April 1863, aged seventy-four, when, it is recorded, '. . . The shops and inns were closed, indeed the whole village mourned the loss of a good and kind friend and master'.[1]

And what became of the Little Bay Mare? One can only presume that she lived on for some years longer in peaceful retirement in the lush, serene fields of Sadborow. Certainly William continued to cherish the horse which, at Salamanca, had carried him 'through the Day delightfully'. The story ends in the summer of 1962. A friend of one of William's descendants mentioned that she was interested in cleaning pictures. By chance one picture (Plate XVII), blackened by age and disinterest, was selected for her from a forgotten attic corner. And in due course the painting yielded its secret: it was—the Little Bay Mare.

Biographical Notes

ALTEN, Victor (?–1820). Lt.-Col. 1st Hussars K.G.L. 1804, which corps he raised. Maj-Gen. 1810. Commanded a cav. bde. in Peninsula 1811–14. Waterloo 1815. His better known brother Charles commanded a bde. in and later the whole of the Light Division.

ANSON, GEORGE. A.D.C. to George III and Col. 1805. Commanded a cav. bde. in Peninsula 1809–13. Maj.-Gen. 1810. G.C.B. 1833. Gen. 1837.

BALLASTEROS, Don Francisco (1770–1832). Col. in Spanish Army at capture of Baylen 1808. Commanded a div. in Andalusia 1811–Sept. 1813, when exiled to Ceuta for objecting to Wellington's appointment as Spanish C.-in-C. Revolutionary leader 1822–3. Condemned to death but escaped to Paris.

BERESFORD, Sir William Carr (1768–1854). Commanded expedition to Buenos Aires 1806. Captured but escaped to England 1807. Gov. and C.-in-C. Madeira 1807–8. Maj.-Gen. with div. at Corunna 1808. Local Lt.-Gen. and Marshal of Port. Army 1809. Reorganized Port. Army with marked success and commanded it until 1819. Cr. Baron 1814. G.C.B. 1815. Cr. Visc. 1823. Gen. 1825. Master Gen. of Ordnance 1828–30. An able administrator with great personal bravery. Wellington's choice as a successor in Graham's absence 1812.

BLAKE, Joachim (1759–1827). Spanish Gen. of Irish extraction. At Albuera 1811. Thereafter worsted in every clash with the French until ignominiously defeated and captured at Valencia Jan. 1812. Active in the Liberal movement of 1820. Died in disgrace.

BOCK, Eberhardt Otto Georg. Of an old military family. Maj.-Gen. 1810. Able Commander of heavy German bde. in Peninsula 1811–14 (Garcia Hernandez 23.7.1812). Temp. commanded all cav. after Cotton wounded. Drowned at sea when returning to England Jan. 1814.

BOWATER, John. Cornet 3rd Dr. 1808. Lieut. 1810. Ret. 1817.

BRANFILL, Champion Edward (1789–1844). Cornet 3rd Dr. May 1810. Lieut. Nov. 1810. Capt. 1813. Ret. 1816.

BROWNE, Francis John (?–1833). Of Frampton, Dorset. M.P. for County 1783–1806. Bequeathed estate to Colquhoun Grant (see below).

BURDETT, Sir Francis (1770–1844). 5th Baronet. M.P. for Westminster from 1807. Ardent parliamentary reformer, opponent of the war against France and critic of the Govt's conduct of it. Attacked existing code of military discipline. Arrested for breach of privilege 1810; 3rd Dr. called to London in case of disturbances.

CAFFARELLI, François-Marie-Auguste (1766–1849). Youngest of five brothers of Italian family long settled in France. Austerlitz 1806. Commanded Army of the North in Spain from 1810 until superseded by Clausel in 1813. With Napoleon in the last battles near Paris 1814. At Metz during the '100 days'. Cr. Peer of France by Louis Philippe.

CALCRAFT, Sir Granby Thomas (1770–1820). Knighted as Lieut. for gallant action at Villiers-en-couche, where 275 cav. beat off 10,000 French, saving the Austrian Emperor Francis II. Lt.-Col. 3rd D.G. 1800. Commanded Regt. in Peninsula 1809–13 (Talavera 1809, Bussaco 1810. Ambushed with Slade April 1812). Maj.-Gen. 1813 but not re-employed. A capable officer but suffered for his anti-Govt. views and those of his brother John (Whig M.P. for Rochester 1806–18).

CARTWRIGHT, William (?–1827). Of Aynhoe, Northants. Col. 3rd Dr. 1807. Lt.-Gen. 1808. Gen. 1819.

CLAUSEL, Bertrand, Comte (1772–1842). Volunteer 1791. Gen. de Div. 1802. Under Junot, Masséna and Marmont 1809–12. Commanded Army of Portugal after Marmont wounded 1812, Army of the North 1813, and a Corps in Soult's Army of Spain 1813–14. Active during the '100 days'. Exiled 1815–20. Charged with Govt. of Algeria 1830. Marshal of France 1831. C.-in-C. Army of Africa 1835–6.

CLINTON, Lord Robert C. St. John (1787–1832). 18th Baron. Capt. 16th Lt. Dr. 1807. Extra A.D.C. to Ld. Wellington in Peninsular War. Brought the Salamanca dispatch and captured trophies to England. Lt.-Col. 1812. Ret. half-pay 1814.

CLOWES, William Legh (1781–1862). Cornet 3rd Dr. 1796. Maj. 1809. Temp. commanded Regt. Oct. 1811–Aug. 1812. Lt.-Col. Aug. 1812. Ret. Dec. 1812. A firm friend of William Bragge in later life.

COTTON, Sir Stapleton (1773–1865). 6th Baronet. Lt.-Col. 25th Lt. Dr. aged 21. Maj.-Gen. 1805. In Peninsula commanding a bde. 1808–9, and all cavalry with ability and vigour 1810–14. Lt.-Gen. and K.B. 1812. Led famous cav. charge at Salamanca; subsequently wounded and on sick leave until mid-1813. Cr. Baron Combermere 1814. G.C.B. 1815. Commanded Allied cav. in France 1815–17. Col. 3rd Dr. 1821–29. C.-in-C. Ireland 1822–25. C.-in-C. East Indies 1825–30 (Bhurtpore 1825). Cr. Visc. 1827. Field Marshal 1855.

Cox, Samuel. Of the Manor House, Beaminster. High Sheriff of Dorset 1809.

CRAUFURD, Robert (1764–1812). Commanded famous Light Bde. (43rd, 52nd and 95th Ft.) from 1809. Maj.-Gen. 1811. Died of wounds storming Ciudad Rodrigo Jan. 1812. An inspiring leader with fearless courage; inclined to be hot-tempered.

CROFT, James, Cornet 3rd D.G. 1810. Capt. 1811. Ret. 1814.

CUMMING, Henry John (?–1856). Lt.-Col. 11th Dr. 1803. Commanded Regt. in Peninsula May 1811–March 1813. Wounded at El Bodon Sept. 1811, where conduct of Regt. was praised by Wellington. Col. 1812. Lt.-Gen. 1830. K.C.H. 1833. Col. 12th Lancers 1837. Gen. 1846.

DIGGENS, Richard (?–1835). Maj. 11th Dr. 1806. Attached to Port. service and commanded 6th Port. Dr. at Vitoria as Brevet Lt.-Col. 1813. Ret. 1820.

DOUGLAS, Sir Howard (1776–1861). 3rd Baronet. Brevet Lt.-Col. 1806. Asst. Q.M.G. at Corunna 1808–9. Brit. Commissioner there 1811–12. Most able observer with Spanish reg. and guerilla forces in Galicia, whose skilful diversions did not allow Marmont to be reinforced before Salamanca. Maj.-Gen. 1821. Gov. of New Brunswick 1823–8. G.C.M.G. 1835. High Commissioner of Ionian Is. 1835–40. Lt.-Gen. 1837. G.C.B. 1841. Gen. 1851. Keenly interested in professional and scientific subjects. F.R.S. 1812. Author of many important military works. His treatise on Naval Gunnery (pub. 1820) led to H.M.S. *Excellent* becoming first gunnery training ship in 1830.

DROUET, Jean Baptiste (1765–1844). Private 1782. Gen. de Brigade 1799. Cr. Comte d'Erlon after Friedland 1807. Mostly in Spain from 1808. Under Soult in Estremadura 1812. Commanded Army of Centre 1813, and a corps under Soult in Army of Spain 1813–14. Commanded French right wing at Waterloo. Self imposed exile until 1830. Gov. of Algeria 1834–6. Marshal of France 1844.

EGERTON, the Rev. Charles. Vicar of Thorncombe July 1790–June 1833.

EGERTON, Charles Bulkeley (?–1857). Lt.-Col. 29th Ft. 1802. In Peninsula 1810–11. Col. 1811. G.C.M.G. 1837. Gen. 1846.

ESPAÑA, Don Carlos (1775–1839). Born a Frenchman d'Espaigne or Espinac. Entered Spanish service 1792. Gen. during Peninsular War. Governor of Madrid during Wellington's occupation. Capt.-Gen. of Catalonia 1818. Viceroy of Navarre 1823. Much involved in the Carlist Wars. Assassinated 1839.

EUSTON, Henry Fitzroy, Earl of (1790–1863). Son and heir of 4th Duke of Grafton. Lieut. 7th Dr. 1810. A.D.C. to Le Marchant

1811–12. Resigned 1812. M.P. for Bury St. Edmonds 1818–20 and 1826–31.

FOWLER, John. Tenant farmer of Forde Grange, 2¼ miles from Sadborow. Buried at Thorncombe 1858, aged eighty-one.

FREMANTLE, John (?–1845). Lieut. and Capt. Coldstream Gds. 1810. Maj. 1813. Lt.-Col. 1814. C.B. 1815. Maj.-Gen. 1841.

GABRIEL, Robert Burd (?–1853). Capt. 2nd D.G. 1805. A.D.C. to Le Marchant 1811 and then Sir W. Stewart 1812–13. Maj.-Gen. and C.B. 1846.

GORDON, James Willoughby (1773–1851). Lt.-Col. 85th Ft. 1801. Mil. Secy. to Duke of York 1804–9. Q.M.G. to Wellington 1812–13. Gross inefficiency led to his removal due to 'ill-health'. Q.M.G. at Horse Guards 1813 until his death; post then abolished for a short period. Maj.-Gen. 1813. Cr. Baronet 1818. G.C.B. 1831. Gen. 1841.

GORE, the Hon. Sanders. Son of 3rd Earl of Arran. Capt. 100th Ft. 1806. Transferred 94th Ft. March 1812. Killed Dec. 1813.

GRAHAM, Sir Thomas (1748–1843). Volunteer at Toulon 1793. Returned to Scotland and raised 90th Ft. Minorca 1798, Ireland 1804–5, A.D.C. to Sir J. Moore at Corunna 1808. Maj.-Gen. commanding a bde. at Walcheren 1809. Lt.-Gen. at Cadiz 1810. Victor of Barrosa 1811, then joined Wellington as 2nd-in-command. Though over sixty, one of Wellington's ablest and most energetic commanders. Corps commander June 1812. Sick leave with eye complaint July 1812–early 1813. Commanded left wing to Vitoria and beyond until Oct. 1813. In command Bergen-op-Zoom expedition Nov. 1813–Feb. 1814. Cr. Baron Lynedoch 1814. G.C.B. 1815. Responsible for founding of United Services Club. Gen. 1821. G.C.M.G. 1837. Died aged ninety-five.

GRANT, Colquhuon (1764–1835). Lt.-Col. commanding 15th Hussars at Corunna 1808. Col. commanding Hussar bde. in Spain Jan.–July 1813, when Regts. were reorganized after Vitoria. Maj.- Gen. 1814. Commanded cav. bde. at Waterloo; several horses killed under him. K.C.B. 1815. Colonel 15th Hussars 1827–35. Lt.-Gen. 1830. Inherited large estates from Francis Browne (see above).

HAMLYN, James. Capt. 7th Lt. Dr. 1813. A.D.C. to Lt.-Gen. Clinton 1814. Maj. and ret. 1823.

HAWKER, Isaac. Tenant on Sadborow estate. Buried at Thorncombe 1831, aged seventy.

HAWKER, Samuel (1763–1838). Lt.-Col. 14th Lt. Dr. 1800. Commanded Regt. in Peninsula 1808–11 (severely wounded at Talavera 1809). Temp. 2nd-in-command of cav. early 1811. A disappointing man; one officer wrote: '. . . [He] was not much better than his chief [Slade] and was objectionable in other respects.' Wellington was equally scathing. Maj.-Gen. Sept. 1811; returned to Woodbridge, not Southampton as believed by W.B. G.C.H. 1836. Gen. 1838.

HERVEY, Felton Bathurst (?–1819). Capt. 14th Lt. Dr. 1803. Lost an arm at the Douro 1809. Lt.-Col. 1810. Badly shaken at Fuentes de Oñoro May 1811. Commanded Regt. with marked distinction from mid–1811, on Col. Hawker's promotion. A.D.C. to Prince Regent and Col. 1814. Wellington's personal staff at Waterloo. C.B. 1815. Cr. Baronet 1818.

HEYWOOD, Arthur. Capt 3rd Dr. 1807. Left for England Dec. 1812. Ret. 1813.

HILL, Sir Rowland (1772–1842). Lt.-Col. 90th Ft. (raised by Graham) 1794. Maj.-Gen. commanding a bde. at Corunna 1808. Commanded 2nd Div. from July 1809 and a corps from Aug. 1811 until end of war with great ability. Wellington had the highest regard for him and 'Daddy' or 'Farmer' Hill was much respected by his troops. Cr. Baron 1814. Corps commander at Waterloo. G.C.B. 1815. 2nd-in-command Army of Occupation in France until Nov. 1818. Gen. 1825. Gen. C.-in-C. 1828–42. Cr. Viscount 1842.

HUTCHINS, Thomas (?–1823), Capt. 3rd Dr. 1805. Le Marchant's brigade-major 1811. A.Q.M.G. after Salamanca. Maj. Dec. 1812. Lt.-Col. 1819.

JACSON, Shalcross. Capt. 3rd Dr. 1810. W.B. attached to his Troop on landing at Lisbon. Ret. 1826. A firm friend of W.B.'s in later life.

JOURDAN, Jean Baptiste (1762–1833). Private in Amer. War of Ind. Rejoined as Lieut. 1792. Gen. 1793. Out of favour 1796–9. Marshal of France 1804. King Joseph's Chief of Staff 1808–13. Cr. Comte 1816. Gov. of Tuileries 1830–3.

KER, John Baker. Lieut. 9th Lt. Dr. 1811. Capt. 1817. Ret. half-pay 1821.

KNIGHT, Edward. Capt. 15th Lt. Dr. 1810. Transferred to Port. service 1812. At Vitoria 1813. Ret. half-pay 1816.

LANGTON, Edward Gore (1789–1860). Lieut. 52nd Ft. 1805. Capt. 1812. Ret. half-pay 1817.

LECOR, Carlos Frederico (1767–1836). Adj. to Mil. Gov. of the Alentejo during 1st Fr. invasion 1807. Went to England and returned with the Royal Lusitanian Legion. One of the most able Port. officers. Brig.-Gen. and Lt.-Gov. of Beira 1811–12. Firmly resisted Marmont's incursion April 1812. Maj.-Gen. commanding 6th Port. bde. at Vitoria and Pyrenees mid–1813. Lt.-Gen.

commanding Allied 7th Div. at Nivelle Nov. 1813, then Independent Port div. until Toulouse 1814. Distinguished service in Brazil from 1817. Captured Montevideo 1817 and Gov. of town until 1828. Cr. Baron 1818, Visc. 1825. Died at Rio de Janeiro.

LE MARCHANT, John Gaspard (1766–1812). Of an old Guernsey family. Lieut. 2nd D.G. 1789. Lt.-Col. 1797. Proposed plan for R.M.A. 1799. Able first Lt.-Gov. of High Wycombe 1801–10. Maj.-Gen. commanding heavy cav. bde. 1811. Killed leading famous charge at Salamanca July 1812. An outstanding officer and great loss to the Army.

MAITLAND, Frederick (1763–1848). In W. Indies most of career 1787–1810. Maj.-Gen. 1805. Brevet Lt.-Gen. and 2nd-in-command in Sicily 1811. Commanded expeditionary force to E. Coast of Spain, landing at Alicante Aug. 1812. Resigned command on ill-health soon after. Lt.-Gov. Dominica 1813. Gen. 1825.

MANNERS, Lord Charles Somerset (1780–1855). 2nd son of 4th Duke of Rutland. Maj. 23rd Lt. Dr. at Corunna 1808. A.D.C. to Wellington 1811–Aug. 1812. Lt.-Col. commanding 3rd Dr. from Aug. 1812. K.C.B. 1813. Lt.-Gen. 1838. Col. 3rd Lt. Dr. 1839. Gen. 1854.

MARMONT. August Frédéric Louis Viesse de (1774–1852). Army officer's son. Napoleon's A.D.C. after Toulon 1796. Gen. de Div. 1800. Gov. of Dalmatia 1805–10. Cr. Duc de Raguse 1808. Marshal of France 1809 (aged thirty-five). Commanded Army of Portugal after Masséna June 1811 until severely wounded at Salamanca July 1812. Later commanded a corps until last battle before Paris 1814. Cr. Peer of France and Maj.-Gen. of Royal Guard after Waterloo. Voluntary exile after 1830 and tutor to Duc de Reichstadt. Died at Venice.

MINA, Don Fransisco Espoz y (1784–1836). Guerilla chief of Navarre 1810–13. Granted rank of Maj.-Gen. and Gov. of Navarre 1813. Much involved in Spain's confused history later. Two periods of exile and raised Navarre to fight against the Carlists until his death.

MUNDY, Godfrey Basil (?–1848). A.D.C. to Lord Charles Fitzroy 1797–1802. Lt.-Col. commanding 3rd Dr. 1803—late 1811, when invalided to England from Lisbon. Gen. 1846. Married the Hon. Sarah Rodney, daughter of Admiral Lord Rodney, 1801. Author of *Life of Lord Rodney*.

MURRAY, Sir John (1768–1827). 8th Baronet. Lt.-Gen. 1812. Commanded Alicante force from Feb. 1813. Barren victory of Castalla April 1813. Expedition to Tarragona mid–1813. Court-martialled for feeble conduct but acquitted 1815. G.C.H. 1817. Gen. 1825. (Col.—Later Maj.-Gen. Sir.—*George* Murray was Wellington's efficient Q.M.G.)

NAPIER, George Thomas (1784–1855). Second of the three famous Napier brothers. A.D.C. to Sir J. Moore at Corunna 1808. Capt. with 52nd in Peninsula 1809–12. Maj. 1811. Commanded Light Div. storming party at Ciudad Rodrigo, losing right arm Jan. 1812. Lt.-Col. 1812. With Regt. again 1814. C.B. 1815. Maj.-Gen. 1837. Gov. and C.-in-C. Cape 1837–43. K.C.B. 1838. Gen. 1854.

O'DONNELL, Henry, Conde d' Abispal (1769–1834). Spanish Gen. of Irish origin. In Royal Guard aged fifteen. One of the more energetic, yet quarrelsome Spanish Gens. Commanded Reserve Army of Andalusia 1813–14 (siege of Pamplona 1813). Imprisoned for not recognizing the Cortes 1814. Released and later Gov. of Cadiz 1822. Much implicated in Liberal uprising. Fled to France.

OGLANDER, Henry. Capt. 47th Ft. 1812. Maj. 1813. Col. 1837. Died 1840.

OGLANDER, Sir William (1769–1852). 6th Baronet, of Parnham, near Beaminster. M.P. for Bodmin 1807–12. Married Maria Anne, eldest daughter of 4th Duke of Grafton, in 1810. (Lord Charles Fitzroy was his uncle by marriage, Lord Euston his brother-in-law.)

PAKENHAM, Edward Michael (1773–1815). Lt.-Col. 64th Ft. 1799. In Peninsula 1809–14. Commanded inf. bde. 1810–11. Local Maj.-Gen. 1811. Commanded 3rd Div., vice Picton, at Salamanca and for entry into Madrid. Adj.-Gen. 1813–14 G.C.B. and killed commanding attempt to take New Orleans 1815. Married Wellington's sister Catherine, in 1806.

PAGET, the Hon. Sir Edward (1775–1849). 4th son of 1st Earl of Uxbridge and brother of Marquess of Anglesey of Waterloo renown. Maj.-Gen. 1805. Commanded reserve at Corunna, lost an arm in advance to Oporto 1809. Lt.-Gen. 1811. Wellington's 2nd-in-command after Graham invalided mid–1812. Captured during retreat from the Tormes Nov. 1812. G.C.B. 1815. Gov. of Ceylon 1821–3. C.-in-C. East Indies 1823–5. Gen. 1825.

PETERBOROUGH and MONMOUTH, Charles Mordaunt, Earl of (c. 1658–1735). Dynamic, courageous soldier and eloquent but erratic statesman. Proposer of English Succession to William of Orange 1686. Commanded an expedition to Spain for Archduke Charles 1705–6. Captured Barcelona 1705, expelled French from Spain 1706, but conduct of War hotly debated in Parliament. Ambassador to various courts 1706–14. K.G. 1713. From his Peninsular exploits, could be regarded to some degree as Wellington's forerunner by a century.

PHELIPS, Edward. 3rd son of the Rev. W. Phelips of Montacute, and Vicar of Yeovil. Lieut. 11th Lt. Dr. 1811. Killed at Waterloo.

PICTON, Thomas (1768–1815). Gov. of Trinidad 1797–1803. His enlightened governorship ended in lengthy court proceedings, from which Wellington got him sent to Peninsula in 1810. Commanded 3rd. Div. with vigour, fearlessness and courage, though not as able as Hill or Graham. A strict disciplinarian. Lt.-Gen. 1811. Wounded at Badajoz April 1812. Invalided to England Aug. 1812–early 1813, then commanded 3rd Div. until 1814. G.C.B., severely wounded at Quatre Bras and killed at Waterloo 1815.

PITT, William Morton. Of Kingston House, near Dorchester. Lt.-Col. Dorset Militia. M.P. for Poole 1780–9 and Dorset 1789–1826.

PLATOFF, Matvai Ivanovich (1751–1818). Russian Count and Gen. Commanded the Cossacks during Retreat from Moscow. At Leipzig 1813. Entered Paris with Russian Army 1815.

POLE, Sir William. 7th Baronet. Of Shute House, near Axminster, Devon (now a girls' school). Sheriff of Dorset 1818–19.

PONSONBY, the Hon. William (1772–1815). 2nd son of 1st Baron Ponsonby; 2nd cousin of Caroline Ponsonby who married Lord Melbourne. Col. 5th D.G. 1810. Commanded Regt. in Peninsula from Sept. 1811, and Le Marchant's bde. after Salamanca July 1812. Maj.-Gen. 1813. K.C.B., and killed at Waterloo commanding Union bde. of heavy cav. 1815.

PORTMAN, Edward Berkeley. Of Bryanston, Dorset. M.P. (with Morton Pitt) for Dorset 1806 until his death in 1823.

SHAKESPEAR, Arthur. Cornet 2nd D.G. 1808. Lieut. 3rd Dr. 1809, A.D.C. to Sir S. Cotton in Peninsula 1811–12. Capt. 10th Lt. Dr. 1814. At Waterloo. Ret. 1818. Author of some entertaining recollections of his army life.

SLADE, John (1762–1859). Col. commanding Hussar bde. at Corunna 1808. Maj.-Gen. commanding a heavy cav. bde. 1809–May 1813. Commanded all cav. in Cotton's absence 1811. Disgraceful ambush June 1812. 'Black Jack' was not a success. One officer who suffered under him wrote: 'As a leader of cavalry he was deplorable. He was a byword for inefficiency throughout the Army.' Lt.-Gen. 1814. Cr. Baronet 1831. G.C.H. 1835. Gen. 1837.

SOMERSET, Lord Robert Edward Henry (1776–1842). 3rd son of 5th Duke of Beaufort and elder brother of Fitzroy, later Lord Raglan of Crimean renown. Lt.-Col. commanding 4th Dr. from

1809. Outstanding at Salamanca July 1812. Maj.-Gen. commanding reformed Hussar bde. July 1813–14. Commanded Household bde. at Waterloo and in France till 1818. G.C.B. 1834. Col. 4th Dr. 1836–42. Gen. 1841.

Spencer, Thomas (1791–1811). Popular and fluent preacher, first near London and after 1800 in Liverpool.

Sturt, Charles (1795–1869). Of an old Dorset family. Ensign 39th Ft. 1813. In Peninsula Feb. 1814–mid–1814. Mil. Sec. to Gov. of New South Wales 1827. Renowned for his explorations of the Murray and Darling river systems 1828–30 and later expeditions 1838 and 1844. Col. Sec. of South Australia 1849–51.

Suchet, Louis Gabriel (1772–1827). Son of a silk manufacturer. Joined army 1792. Made reputation in Italy. Gen. de Div. 1799. In Spain 1808–14, commanding French armies on E. Coast from 1810. Cr. Duc d'Albufera and Marshal of France 1811. Captured Valencia 1812. With Soult in final days of war 1814. Cr. Peer of France by Louis XVIII; deprived of title after activity in the '100 days'.

Thoyts, John. Capt. Royal Horse Guards 1805. Lt.-Col. 1815. Ret. 1820.

Tounsend, John (?–1845). Lieut. 14th Lt. Dr. 1806. With Regt. in Peninsula from 1808. Capt. 1811. Taken prisoner March 1814. Lt.-Col. 1829. A.D.C. to Queen Victoria and Col. commanding Regt. in India 1841 until leave early 1845.

Vandeleur, John Ormsby (1763–1849), Maj.-Gen. commanding bde. in Light Div. in Peninsula 1811. Badly wounded at Ciudad Rodrigo Jan. 1812. At Salamanca 1812 and Vitoria 1813. Commanded a cav. bde. at Waterloo; commanded all cav. after Lord Uxbridge wounded. Lt.-Gen. 1821. Col. 14th Lt. Dr. 1823–30. G.C.B. 1833. Gen. 1838.

Whitbread, Samuel (1765–1815). Son of founder of well-known brewery family. M.P. for Bedford from 1790. Supporter of Fox and later active, eloquent, independent opponent of Govt. From 1810, chairman of committee for rebuilding Drury Lane theatre after its disastrous fire.

Wilson, Sir Robert Thomas (1777–1849). Cornet 15th Dr.; knighted with Sir G. Calcraft for gallant action at Villiers-en-couche 1794. Raised and commanded Royal Lusitanian Legion 1808. In Peninsula until 1810. Col. 1810. Brit. Mil. Correspondent at Allied armies' H.Q. 1812–14. Maj.-Gen. 1813. Dismissed for alleged disrespect at Queen Caroline's funeral 1821. Re-instated as Lt.-Gen. 1825. Active M.P. for Southwark 1818, 1820 and 1826. Succeeded Grant as Col. 15th Hussars 1835. Gov. and C.-in-C. Gibraltar 1842–9.

WORCESTER, Henry, Marquess of (1792–1853). Eldest son of 6th Duke of Beaufort; later 7th Duke. Lieut. 10th Lt. Dr. 1811. A.D.C. to Wellington 1812–14. Maj. 37th Ft. 1819. Resigned 1832. M.P. for Monmouth 1813-32; W. Gloucestershire 1835. A Lord of the Admiralty 1815–19. K.G. 1842.

Bibliography

Ainslie. *History of the Royal Dragoons* (1887).

Anglesey. *The Capel Letters* (1955).

Army Lists. Years 1800–1845.

Arthur. *Story of the Household Cavalry*, vol. i (1909).

Bragge. Unpublished MSS. (Ed. R. Grosvenor Bartelot, 1901).

Bridge and Lowndes. *The Selective Traveller in Portugal* (revised edn. 1958).

Burke. *Landed Gentry*. Various Years.

Cannon. *Historical Record of the 3rd Dragoons* (1837).

Cannon. *Historical Record of the 4th Dragoon Guards* (1837).

Cannon. *Historical Record of the 5th Dragoon Guards* (1837).

Combermere. *Memoirs and Correspondence of F.M. Viscount Combermere* (1866).

Dictionary of National Biography.

Dillon. *Narrative* (Ed. Lewis). Navy Records Society, No. 98 (1957).

Donaldson. *The Eventful Life of a Soldier* (1827).

Dorset County Chronicle 18 April 1863.

D'Urban. *Peninsular Journal* (Ed. Rousseau, 1930).

Ford. *Handbook for Spain* (9th edn. 1898).

Fortescue. *History of the British Army*, vols. viii and ix (1917–20).

Foster's *Peerage*, 1881.

Foy. *Guerre de la Peninsule*, vol. i (Paris, 1827).

Foy. *Vie Militaire de Général Foy.* (Ed. Girod de l'Ain, Paris, 1900).

General Regulations for the Army, 1811.

Gomm. *Letters and Journals of F. M. Sir W. Gomm* (1881).

Grattan. *Adventures with the Connaught Rangers* (1847).

Gronow. *The Reminiscences and Recollections of Captain Gronow* (Ed. Greco, 1892).

Guedalla. *Palmerston* (1926).

Hamilton. *Historical Record of the 14th (King's) Hussars* (1901).

Hansard. 8 March 1813.

Hutchins. *History of Dorset*, vol. iv (3rd edn. 1873).

Keith, *The Keith Papers*, vol. iii, (Ed. Lloyd). Navy Records Society No. 96 (1955).

Larpent. *The Private Journal of Judge Advocate Larpent*, vol. ii (1853).

Le Marchant. *Memoirs of the late Maj.-Gen. Le Marchant* (1841).

Liddell. *The Xth Hussars* (1891).

Lock. *Western Rebellion* (1912).

Marshall. *Western Martyrology* (1705).

Napier. *The History of the War in the Peninsula,* vol. iv (1834–40).

Norman. *Battle Honours of the British Army* (1911).

Oman. *History of the Peninsular War,* vols. iv–vii (1902–31).

Paget. *Letters and Memorials of Gen. the Hon. Sir Edward Paget* (1898).

Public Records Office: W.O. 1/251, 253; W.O. 17/21, 256, 271, 2471, 2475; W.O. 25/1398.

Pomeroy. *History of the 5th Dragoon Guards* (1924).

Pulman. *Book of the Axe* (4th Ed., 1874).

Royal Kalendar 1780–1830.

Smyth. *History of the XXth.*

Somerset Archaeological Society Proceedings, vol xxviii (1882).

The Complete Baronetage, vols. i–v (1909).

The Complete Peerage.

The Royal Military Calendar (1820).

The Times 11 June 1811, 31 July 1812, 26 September 1812, 13 March 1813.

Tompkinson. *The Diary of a Cavalry Officer* (1894).

Wellington. *Dispatches and General Orders of Field Marshal the Duke of Wellington* (Ed. Gurwood, 1834–8).

Wellington. *Supplementary Dispatches of the Duke of Wellington* (Ed. 2nd Duke of Wellington, 1858–72).

Williams. *Historical Records of the 11th Hussars* (1908).

Notes and References

PROLOGUE

1. *Somerset Archaeological Proceedings,* vol xxviii, ii, p. 57.
2. Marshall, *Western Martyrology,* p. 166.

CHAPTER ONE: WIMBLEDON COMMON TO CIUDAD RODRIGO

1. *The Times,* 11 June 1811.
2. Guedalla, *Palmerston,* p. 49.
3. Wellington, *Dispatches and General Orders,* vol. vii, pp. 231–2.
4. Every care had been taken during the sea voyage to keep the horses in condition. Four horses at a time had been exercised in the hold for a quarter of an hour each day. Their feet had then been washed and their legs rubbed.
5. The old riding school is now the Museum of Royal Coaches. The Regent of Portugal had sailed to Brazil before the first invasion in November 1807.
6. The incident affecting Col. Hervey occurred at the Battle of Fuentes de Oñoro. He had already lost an arm. His leg on this occasion was certainly saved by a thick book, although the Regimental historian ascribes the honour to *Quenedo's Works.*
7. The 11th Light Dragoons lost a strong picquet near Elvas on 9 June. One officer and 10 men were surprised near the Perales Pass on 15 August. Eleven days later a picquet was attacked near Ciudad Rodrigo.
8. Le Marchant did not, in fact, return to England. His wife had died suddenly but he declined the offer to return home as his family was happily cared for in Guernsey.
9. One hundred deaths were recorded for the week ending 15 September.
10. Major Dickson fully described the formidable task of bringing up the siege train for Ciudad Rodrigo in his journal. The ordnance depôt at Vila da Ponte, 70 miles from the town, was completed by 20 September.
11. W.B. was right in doubting Col. Mundy's news. It was Gen. Freire, to whose aid Blake had taken two divisions after Albuera, who had been soundly beaten by Soult near Granada on 9–10 August.

12. The prescription was probably that of John Moncrief, given in his *The Poor Man's Physician* (2nd edn. pub. 1716). 'Dysenteria: A bloody Flux. It is stopt chiefly with an infusion of Rhubarb in Rose and Plantain Water.'

13. *The Geographical, Historical and Commercial Grammar* (pub. 1770) was the most renowned work of William Guthrie (1708–70), parliamentary reporter and author of various ambitious literary efforts.

14. The widespread sickness of the Army is shown in the Weekly State of 15 October:

	British	Portuguese
Effective	35,200	24,125
Detached	3,451	3,112
Sick (present)	1,701	1,108
Sick (absent)	15,759	5,454

15. On 15 October, the 4th Dragoon Guards had 167 sick in hospital and 30 in quarters. Sixty horses were transferred the previous week.

16. The 11th Light Dragoons and 1st German Hussars had repeatedly charged four French cavalry regiments at El Bodon on 26 September. The 5th Foot at one stage had charged the French Dragoons.

    Napier credits the cavalry with charging 'not once but twenty times'. Oman's figure of eight or nine times is more plausible.

    The conduct of these two regiments was commended as 'an example to be followed in all circumstances' in Lord Wellington's General Order of 2 October.

    [Napier, *War in the Peninsula*, vol. iv, p. 239, Wellington, *Dispatches and General Orders*, vol. vii, pp. 434–5.]

17. Of the 2,600 French caught in Arroyo Molinos, only about 500 escaped. Gen. Bron—the 2nd-in-command—and Prince Aremberg were among the Prisoners.

    Napoleon was so furious with Girard over this affair, that he temporarily deprived him of his command. Meanwhile Hill was recommended for a K.B.

18. Spanish guerillas seized over 200 cattle belonging to the garrison of Ciudad Rodrigo as they were grazing on the glacis on 15 October. The Governor, Gen. Renouard—a Swiss—was also captured in trying to recover them. His brother was then Vice Master of Trinity College, Cambridge.

19. A comet of particular beauty was visible for several weeks in the autumn of 1811. To it was ascribed later the outstanding quality of that year's vintage of port wine!

20. Combermere, *Memoirs and Correspondence*, vol. i, p. 296.
21. Although the Spaniards would have liked Wellington to believe this good news from Valencia, he allowed himself no illusions as his Dispatches to Lord Liverpool dated 4 and 18 December show . . . 'Reports of this description have generally been the forerunner of . . . some serious disaster.' . . .

    Valencia fell to the French on 9 January. Wellington heard of this the day he captured Ciudad Rodrigo.
22. Four Divisions were ordered to make fascines and gabions in mid-December.
23. As a sop to the Spaniards, who had asked for the attention of the French to be diverted from Gen. Ballasteros in the mountains north of Gibraltar and from the garrison at Tarifa, Hill was ordered forward to Merida on 18 December.
24. The Badajoz rumour probably arose because five regiments of Poles were being withdrawn (with the Imperial Guards) in preparation for Napoleon's Russian offensive.
25. Following Napoleon's orders, some baffling counter-marching had been taking place. Marmont had to send a third of his force to help Suchet reduce Valencia. The division in the Tagus valley marched eastwards in mid-December together with other units. It was this momentary depletion of the Army of Portugal which gave Wellington the chance to capture Ciudad Rodrigo.
26. Col. Mundy and 3 men of the 3rd Dragoons were invalided home in early November. Fifteen more men followed in early December.
27. At Ciudad Rodrigo about 1,700 of all ranks, including Gen. Barrié, the Governor, were taken prisoner. The exact numbers are uncertain for Wellington's figures exceeded the garrison strength by the French returns. The latter were, however, not above suspicion. One authority has stated there were 1,360 un-wounded prisoners.
28. The allies lost 125 killed and 425 wounded in the assault. Gen. Craufurd was shot through the lungs and died 48 hours later. He was buried at the foot of the breach where he fell.
29. Wellington ordered Hill to withdraw to the Portalegre-Castelo Branco area on 9 January. There he was better placed to prevent any French move to ease the pressure on Ciudad Rodrigo.

CHAPTER TWO: CAVALRY SCREEN FOR BADAJOZ

1. W.B's remark on men joining the Regiment led by a Brunswick officer is obscure. The incident is not recorded elsewhere.
2. Wellington did not, in fact, visit Cadiz.

3. W.B. would have missed Lord Charles Manners. He returned to England on sick leave in H.M.S. *Leopard* in early January.

4. W.B. did not miss anything. Incessant torrential rain at the beginning of February not only prevented Lord Wellington's Meet but also more serious work. The trestle bridge over the Agueda carried away and the suburbs of Ciudad Rodrigo were badly flooded.

5. The 4th Dragoon Guards were brigaded with the 3rd Dragoon Guards and 1st Royal Dragoons under Slade.

6. Owing to the weak condition of the draft oxen, only sixteen howitzers could be sent south from Ciudad Rodrigo. The new siege train comprised these, the sixteen 24-pdrs. seen by W.B. (landed at Setubal at the end of January) and twenty Russian 18-pdrs., ill-matched to English shot, which were lent by the Royal Navy from the Lisbon arsenal.

7. Vila Viçosa was the 'Sandringham' of the Braganzas. Carlos I spent his last night there before being assassinated in 1908. The Chase or Tapada of some 4,200 acres, whose charms were sung by Lope de Vega, is enclosed by a wall 18 Kilometres—not miles —long.

8. The numbers of the French at Llerena is open to doubt. 1,800 men, and three battalions with two cavalry regiments have both been mentioned.

9. D'Urban, Beresford's Chief of Staff, who was present at this night incident, also recorded some scathing remarks in his diary. See also page 47.

10. Drouet lay to the East with 12,000. Soult was advancing from Cadiz with 13,000 to relieve Badajoz. Even so, Sir S. Cotton was handsomely dined by the Spaniards in Azuaga on 30 March.

11. At La Granja on 1 April, two squadrons of 3rd Dragoons were attacked by seven French squadrons and some infantry under the supposed personal direction of Soult. A man is reputed to have deserted the previous evening and to have given information. The Regiment lost 1 man killed, 12 taken prisoner and 12 horses killed. See also page 48.

12. Wellington's intentions were for two divisions to continue investing Badajoz, while the rest of the Army met Soult at Albuera.

13. Oman, *History of the Peninsular War*, vol. v, p. 269.

14. Oman, *History of the Peninsular War*, vol. v, p. 615.

15. Bridge and Lowndes, *The Select Traveller in Portugal*, p. 21.

16. The cavalry encounter at Llerena on 11 April cost the British 58 casualties. W.B's figures for the 5th Dragoon Guards and the

French are correct. The French force at Llerena probably did not exceed 12,000.

17. The Badajoz scaling ladders were 30 feet long and very heavy. The Sadborow windows are 25 feet above the ground.

18. W.B.'s figures can be read two ways. The 4th Division (five regts.) lost 81 officers in the assault. The famed Light Division lost 63 officers at Badajoz and 15 at Ciudad Rodrigo, in all 78.

19. The whole Army was even more widely dispersed in early May— from the Douro in the north to Elvas in the south. Hill's corps totalled nearer 11,000.

20. Wellington had contemplated an invasion of Andalusia *before* Marmont's thrust into lower Beira. During April Graham had been told to spread reports in Zafra of an impending offensive. Soult remained firmly under the impression that invasion was imminent for a long time, due to the Allies' deceptive dispositions.

21. The explanation follows in Chapter 3, Notes 1 and 2.

CHAPTER THREE: SALAMANCA AND BURGOS: TRIUMPH AND RETREAT

1. Hill's nervous rearguard commander had called out not only the 3rd Dragoons but also Graham's 1st and 6th divisions when Slade's outposts were pushed in near Zafra and a large reconnaissance force closed to within 60 miles of the bridge wreckers at Almaraz.

2. Slade's Brigade, in following up the French, lost 22 killed, 26 wounded and 118 taken prisoner when set upon in a defile about 12 miles north-east of Llerena on 11 June.

   Wellington was so furious that he made the stinging and much quoted remark about cavalry officers being unable apparently to manoeuvre except on Wimbledon Common.

   Slade retained his command until May 1813. The Luddites were particularly active in early 1812.

3. The fort comprised three closely grouped fortified convents. An attack on the two smaller ones failed on 23 June. The largest was fired on 27th.

4. Wellington recorded that thirteen out of twenty-five convents and twenty out of twenty-five colleges had been destroyed in Salamanca.

5. Hill and Ballasteros were to press upon Soult alternately so as to prevent his marching north. Hill advanced to Llerena in mid-June to relieve the pressure on Ballasteros. Soult thought this was the beginning of an invasion of Andalusia—even on the day Wellington was crossing the Agueda.

The siege of Cadiz lingered on for two more months. In May, Soult's field force mustered only 24,000 out of a possible 54,000.

6. Wellington had planned a landing in Catalonia. He was thwarted by Lord Bentink in Sicily whose preoccupation in other feeble schemes prevented an ill-managed force from reaching Spain until late July. After more delays the force landed at Alicante on 9 August—too few, too late and in the wrong place.

7. The Spanish force making for Zamora only reached the Esla on 1 July. A Portuguese cavalry brigade got to a point north-east of the town the following day.

8. Wellington had decided upon Beresford as his successor if needed, because of his wider views and organizing ability.

9. There were two bankers in Lombard St.: Stephenson, Remington & Co., at No. 69, and Stevenson & Salt of No. 80. W.B. mentions in Letters 8 and 16 that his drafts were drawn on Stevenson instead of Stephenson (as in Letter 12), so that was the most likely mistake.

10. The Allies lost 99 killed and 331 wounded in taking the Salamanca forts.

11. On the heights of San Christobal, Wellington had remarked 'damned tempting' but had refused to be drawn, since he wanted Marmont to attack his strong defensive position.
[Fortescue, *History of the British Army*, vol. viii, p. 462.]

12. The sorry tale in Salamanca was exaggerated. A number of soldiers and 20 civilians were killed and some houses were wrecked when barrels of powder from the captured forts were blown up accidentally by one of Don Carlos's officers.

13. Besides soldiers of both armies swimming together in the Douro, they treated each other to wine and brandy!

14. Combermere, *Memoirs and Correspondence*, vol. i, p. 275.

15. Wellington ordered Packenham to 'move on with the 3rd Division, take those heights in your front—and drive everything before you' at about a quarter to four. Orders to the rest of the army followed.
[Grattan, *Adventures with the Connaught Rangers*, pp. 241–2.]

16. Wellington wrote of Le Marchant that he had to regret the loss of a most able officer. The officer killed with him was probably Lieut. Selby, the only officer casualty of the 3rd Dragoons. Besides Selby the Regiment lost 10 men killed, 9 wounded and 32 horses. Lord E. Somerset, commanding the 4th Dragoons, captured five guns single-handed.

17. The attack by four squadrons of Bock's Germans on three French squares at Garcia Hernandez was described by Gen. Foy as 'the

boldest and most gallant cavalry charge of the whole war in Spain'. W.B.'s figure for prisoners taken may be a little high but exact numbers are not known.

[Foy, *Guerre de la Peninsule*, vol. i, pp. 290–1.]

18. W.B.'s figures are amazingly accurate for a junior officer so soon after the battle.

Allied losses at Badajoz: 4,670 (3,605 British).

Allied losses at Salamanca: 4,762 (3,129 British).

French losses at Salamanca: Estimated only. Napoleon was told 12,000. A fair minimum was 14,000.

Accepted trophies list: 20 guns, 2 eagles and 6 colours.

19. Marmont was badly hit in the right arm and side by a shell at about half past four.

20. By implication W.B. is a little unfair to Sir Stapelton. He was wounded *after* the battle when his party was returning from Alba de Tormes at 11 p.m. and was mistaken for a body of the enemy by a Portuguese picquet. He had to spend the night in a pig trough.

21. On the initiative of Major Clowes, the 3rd Dragoons went to help Alten's brigade in a confused action near Castrillo and beat off a brigade of French Dragoons. The Regiment lost 4 men killed and 4 wounded.

22. The freak thunderstorm on the eve of the battle has been widely recorded. One officer and 17 men of the 3rd Dragoons had to be sent to the rear after the stampede. Twenty men of the 5th Dragoon Guards were disabled.

23. The death of Marmont, Bonnet and Beresford was a rumour only. All three were seriously wounded.

24. Wellington has been much criticized for halting at Flores d'Avila instead of persuing a demoralized army. Supplies had to catch up though, and with Cotton disabled, Le Marchant killed and Bock's Germans exhausted, he was without a trusted cavalry commander.

25. The official figures were 800 sick and seventeen guns.

26. About 10 miles from Madrid, the Portuguese cavalry forsook their commander in the face of some 4,000 French, leaving four guns to their mercy. Bock's brigade was bivouacking but quickly galloped into action, supported by Ponsonby's, and the French were driven off. The guns were retaken but this 'devil of an affair'—as Wellington called it—cost the Allies 53 men killed, 98 wounded, 45 taken prisoner and 81 horses lost.

[Fortescue, *History of the British Army*, vol viii, p. 559.]

27. Ford, *Handbook of Spain*, pp. 86–87.

28. Apathy in Valladolid stemmed from suffering three occupations in six weeks. The proclamation of the March 1812 Constitution from the Town Hall was poorly attended.

29. W.B. had been doing some astute eavesdropping. Soult had received a second angry letter from Joseph telling him to evacuate Andalusia or resign. Even before he received it, he had given up the siege of Cadiz and begun marching for Valencia. He was at Cordoba on 30 August. Wellington heard this on 8 September —the date of W.B.'s letter—and at once ordered Hill to come north across the Tagus at Almaraz.

30. W.B. was alluding to standards of behaviour and scholarship. Laura was the name given to a group of cells inhabited by ascetics in the earliest monastic communities in the East. St. Arsenius (c. A.D. 354–450) was renowned for his knowledge of Greek and Roman literature.

31. Major Clowes was not mentioned in Wellington's dispatches covering the Castrillo action and Salamanca, although all the other cavalry brigade and regimental commanders were. One explanation is that Wellington was not sure who was in command of the 3rd Dragoons on those days. Lord Charles Manners's appointment was dated 2 *July* but he only assumed command on *8 August*.

32. Wellington was waiting for the Galician army to join him.

33. Ten thousand Galicians under Castaños reached Burgos on 16 September, which made the French withdraw. The Spaniards had been 12 miles away on the 12th but had slavishly stuck to their orders to march via Valladolid.

34. The interchange on 'Justice done them' is interesting and not recorded elsewhere. There were 421 casualties (204 Highlanders). Wellington wrote: 'If I had had some troops who have stormed before, I should not have lost a fourth of the number.'
[Wellington, *Dispatches and General Orders*, vol. ix, pp. 443–4.]

35. Wellington was acutely short of both guns and ammunition. One battery of two 18-pdrs. and three howitzers was ready on 22nd, on which day two galleries were begun.

36. The Morning State of 24 September showed 19,876 Allied sick. From Cordoba Soult had marched to Granada. He left the town to join Joseph on 16 September, taking 6,000 sick with him.

37. Orders for the final attempt on Burgos castle were issued p.m. 18 October, the date of W.B.'s letter.

38. Wellington's siege train comprised three 18-pdrs.—originally loaned from the Lisbon naval arsenal for use at Badajoz—and five 24-pdr. howitzers. These opposed nine heavy guns, eleven

field pieces and six mortars. 'Nelson' was the only fully service-able gun after 18 October.

39. W.B. was twelfth in seniority in August 1811, but only nine Lieutenants landed with the Regiment.

40. A charming notice appeared in *The Times* of 26 September 1812, in which Morton Pitt stated his intention to stand for Parliament in spite of his bereavement. He was M.P. for Dorset until 1826.

41. Lord Charles was referring to the Prince Regent. On his mar-riage, Leigh Hunt had written an article in his brother's paper, the *Examiner*, in which he said of the Prince 'this Adonis in loveliness was a corpulent man of fifty'. Both the Hunts were fined £500 and imprisoned for two years.

42. D'Urban, *Peninsular Journal*, p. 301.

43. Sir E. Paget only recorded that he was taken by 3 Chasseurs à cheval of the 10th Regiment.

44. Torrential rain fell during the night after the French had crossed the Tormes which made the river impassable. Wellington wrote that had it rained 24 hours earlier, he could have held his cantonments by Salamanca.

45. Wellington was appointed C.-in-C. of all the Spanish forces in September. In a manifesto Ballasteros deplored the appointment as an insult to the Spanish army. He was promptly replaced and exiled to Ceuta. Ballasteros's inactivity in the south during the summer was one of many reasons which forced Wellington back to the Agueda.

Don Carlos de España had not been superseded but he was always a sharp rogue to deal with.

46. The 3rd Dragoons probably made use of the Germans' supplies on 16 November, when the 1st Hussars were attacked by the French.

47. Caffarelli had returned to Burgos. Other French units moved down the Douro to re-establish garrisons at Zamora and Toro.

48. Foy, *Vie Militaire de Général Foy*, p. 193.

CHAPTER FOUR: PORTUGAL TO THE PYRENEES

1. W.B. was doubtless reminded of his uncle's fatal accident. For an after dinner wager at Forde Abbey he had jumped across a pond and landed heavily in a rabbit hole on the far side, fractur-ing his ankle, from which he died a week later.

2. Wellington's Memorandum of 28 November was written in strong and general terms. It was deeply resented in many regi-ments where discipline had not wavered in spite of fearful

privations. There are indications that Wellington was not aware that the commissariat arrangements had been so grossly misdirected.

How this confidential Memorandum reached the English newspapers is a mystery but Col. Gordon was deeply suspected.

Wellington suffered from Horse Guards nominated officers until after the Battle of Vitoria. He remarked: 'What a situation is mine! It is impossible to prevent incapable men from being sent out to the army; and when I complain that they have been sent, I am to be responsible!'

[Wellington, *Dispatches and General Orders*, vol. x, p. 34.]

3. Without any previous consultation, Col. Gordon had replaced Wellington's trusted Q.M.G., Col. George Murray. Wellington's *Cri de coeur* in the above note applied only too well to the former. Not only was he incompetent but he also corresponded secretly with Opposition leaders. His recall was 'arranged' in January 1813, albeit to become Q.M.G. at the Horse Guards, where he continued to weave a peculiar web in politics and 'interest'.

4. On 25 January 1813, the 3rd Dragoons had 94 sick. The total British sick amounted to 17,500.

5. The 4th Dragoon Guards had a sad Peninsular record; the Regiment never recovered from its heavy sickness in October 1811. See also Chapter 1, Notes 7 and 15.

6. A hospital of wooden cottages was being put up by Castelo Rodrigo—part of many plans to improve the Army's health.

7. Caffarelli was superseded by Clausel in January 1813. Soult was recalled a month later.

8. Col. Grant's brigade (10th, 15th and 18th Hussars) reached Lisbon in early February 1813.

9. Lord Wellesley's motion censured the Government for its inefficient prosecution and feeble support of his brother's campaign of 1812.

10. W.B.'s observation is ingenious for there does not appear to be any other reference to this intercepted dispatch. Soult may well have written it before his recall while the French armies were being regrouped, for the dispositions concern the Army of the South.

Wellington was never in the habit of recording for his superiors all his intelligence, so something of this kind was quite probable.

11. Joseph had left Madrid for good on 17 March. News of Sir J. Murray's barren victory at Castalla on 13 April had not yet reached Wellington.

12. The 4th and 7th Divisions were also part of Graham's force but had still to reach the assembly area.
Wellington crossed the Agueda with the Light Division and three cavalry brigades on 22 May. Hill's corps, marching from Bejar, joined him on 24th. Salamanca was occupied on 27th.

14. Only 45,000 infantry and 10,000 cavalry could oppose Wellington immediately. Given time, a further 30,000 could have been assembled.

15. W.B. would have received the long awaited box of clothes as well, for the following quaint letter to his father has been preserved: Belem 16th June 1813.

> Sir
> I received your Kind letter this Day Dated Sadborow June 1st and in answer I have to inform you that I Received the Box you Mentioned on the 22nd April and I had an opportunity of Forwarding to Mr William, on the 27th April by a Sargeant Harner of our Regement which gave me Grate Pleashure, I having Received a Letter from Lt Bragge Two or Three day Befare on that head which I make no Dout befare this time he as it Safe in his Possession. Should I at any Futer time Receve anaything addressed to Lt Bragge I shall Loose no time in aquainting im of it and act agreeable to his Orders.
> I have the Hanor to be Sir, your Most Obedient and Humble Servant
>
> N. Leigh.   T.S.Major 3d/ or K.O. Drags.

16. The Household Cavalry brought the first of the Prince Regent's gaudy uniform changes to the Peninsula. One parliamentary critic had ridiculed the innovations as: 'Nothing could be more absurd . . . they were worthy of Grimaldi; adorned as they were in all their pantomimic pomp and feathers, they looked like the Rinaldos of an epic poem.' [Hansard, 8 March 1813.]
When the Household Cavalry landed at Lisbon, they had thrown away their curry combs and brushes, thinking them unnecessary impedimenta on Service.

17. Ponsonby's brigade totalled 1,398 on 25 May.

18. In January 1813, Napoleon had ordered 25 picked men from each battalion or cavalry regiment to be sent back to France to reform the Imperial Guard after the disastrous retreat from Moscow. The 7th Polish Lancers was the last Polish regiment to leave Spain.

19. The precise French numbers before Vitoria are not known but have been estimated as 57,000–58,000 with a large, useless 'tail' attending to the baggage train,

20. Total Allied losses were 5,158 (3,675 British). The French fought hard to keep the Gamarra Mayor bridge until the general withdrawal made it untenable. The bridge cost both sides about 1,000 casualties in all.

21. The official return, dated also 24 June, shows 151 guns, 100 artillery wagons and about 2,000 prisoners taken.

22. After the Tierra de Campos, rich in corn but devoid of water, the Ebro valley could hardly support the large, concentrated army, though water was now plentiful. It was a remarkable feat of the commissariat to feed 80,000 in so small an area—something which has never received the prominence it deserved.

23. See also Note 26, below.

24. The tale runs that Lieut. Lord Worcester and Capt. Wyndham, leading their squadron of 10th Hussars, fired into Joseph's carriage. He only had time to throw himself out and escape on horseback, covered by a troop of horse.

25. Ponsonby's and Grant's brigades were involved in an encounter on the heights of Estepar, 10 miles south-west of Burgos on 12 June. W.B.'s remark shows that Wellington withdrew the cavalry before they attacked the French rearguard. This conforms with his belief (in spite of Garcia Hernandez) that cavalry could not overwhelm formed units of infantry.

   The 3rd Dragoons lost 1 officer and 1 man wounded, and 8 horses. For the incident in 1812, see page 76.

26. Clausel first heard news of the battle p.m. on 22nd. Wellington knew he was more than a day's march from Vitoria on the eve of the battle from a loyal innkeeper who had ridden some 40 miles to give this useful information. Clausel's (and Suchet's) absence assured Wellington's numerical superiority and was an added reason for his attacking at once on the 21st.

27. It was a popular belief at the time that Clausel acted on this legendary Alcade's information. In fact he had resolved much earlier to make for Saragossa as fast as possible. This is borne out by his destroying two bridges over the Ebro to thwart the Allies.

28. There appears to have been more than just professional inefficiency in the reshuffle of the Hussar regiments. Grant's brigade had been one of the two cavalry brigades actively engaged at Vitoria, and the first to come upon the baggage train.

   Wellington expressed his wrath over the looting and plundering which had taken place after the battle in one dispatch, adding: 'The –th are a disgrace to the name of a soldier. . . . I propose to draft their horses from them and send the men to England, if I cannot get the better of them in any other manner.' [Wellington, *Dispatches and General Orders*, vol. x. p. 473.]

29. Paris was pushed out of Saragossa by the Spaniards on 10 July. He found the road to Jaca the only one open to him and he reached the town on the 13th. His 5,000 men ultimately joined Soult's left wing, in France—a serious loss to Suchet.

Suchet intended marching to Saragossa, but with Paris ousted and the Allies back near Pamplona, there was no object in leaving Tortosa.

30. O'Donnell's army of 11,000—the discrepancy in numbers is accounted for later—relieved Hill's corps, which had begun to march up the Bastan valley earlier in the month. Pamplona was ultimately starved into submission by the Spaniards.

31. The Commander at Roncesvalles had written a dejected dispatch to Wellington, in which he presumed he would have to make for Vitoria if forced to retreat past Pamplona.

32. A furious thunderstorm broke over the Pyrenees on the eve of the first battle of Sorauren—as at Salamanca and at Waterloo yet to come. Wellington's dramatic arrival at the eleventh hour (a.m.) on the 27th after a gruelling ride from his H.Q. at Lesaca was greeted by wild cheering from all units, led by the Portuguese with the cry: 'Douro!' The reassuring effect was complete. Soult postponed his attack until the following day, by which time his opportunity had been lost.

33. The 6th Division, marching from well to the left of the Allied army that morning, reached its battle position just after noon. The three fires were from two brigades of the 6th Division on the left and centre and the 4th Division on the right of the valley leading to Sorauren.

34. Casualties in the nine day Pyrenean campaign were:
    Allies: 7,000 (4,700 British).
    French: 13,500 killed, wounded or captured.
    8,000–10,000 stragglers who rejoined their units later.

35. Neither Joseph nor Jourdan ever reached Paris. Joseph was retired to his estate of Morfontaine, on condition that he did not visit Paris, with imprisonment waiting if he intrigued. Jourdan retired to his estate of Coudray near Orleans.

36. The bombardment of San Sebastian began on 26 August. There had been enough guns for some time but adequate powder and shot only arrived from England on the 23rd.

37. Don Carlos occupied O'Donnell's posts before Pamplona when the latter was called out for the Battles of Sorauren. A worse character he proved to be: he ended his days with a millstone round his neck in the River Segre—a compliment for his repressive régime as Capt. Gen. of Catalonia.
38. See also Note 34, above.
39. In August one new infantry brigade from England and the 1st Guards brigade from Oporto joined the Army.
40. Soult was merely regrouping after his nine-day venture.
41. When Paris moved out of Saragossa on 10 July, he left a small garrison in the citadel. Mina surrounded it the same day but did not bombard until 1 August. The French surrendered after the walls had crumbled and they had blown up the magazine. 500 prisoners were marched out.
42. It is gratifying to note that Ponsonby's brigade had ridden through the orgy of plunder after Vitoria without a man leaving the ranks. One suspects that Grant was susperseded by Somerset for this 'activity' as much as for any other reason.

CHAPTER FIVE: INTO FRANCE

1. Wellington, *Dispatches and General Orders,* vol. xi, p. 384.
2. Phelps was a Thorncombe man; a large family of that name lived in the village. Nothing more is known about him.
3. W.B., being so far in rear, was rather out of touch. Cotton still commanded all the cavalry only, even if the numbers had increased.

   Cotton felt he should have received a title after Salamanca, where he was nominally 2nd-in-command. Wellington was adamant because of the delicate position of Beresford—a Portuguese Marshal but more junior British General. During his sick leave in England, he had pressed his claim without success. He received a Barony at the end of the war.

   Gen. Paris only commanded his brigade—those men he had brought with him from Saragossa.

   See also Chapter 4, Note 29.
4. Wellington sent back all the Spanish troops, less one division, beyond the Bidassoa by mid-November 1813. It was a painful decision as he revealed in one dispatch: '. . . Without food or pay they must plunder; and if they plunder, they will ruin us all.'

   Certain units were brought forward for the closing stages of the campaign—fed by Wellington.
   [Wellington, *Dispatches and General Orders,* vol. xi, pp. 306–7.]

5. On 25 January 1814, the 3rd Dragoons had only 12 sick, all but 2 being 'present'. A month later there were 9 sick.

6. For the past decade, John MacArthur, the 'Father' of New South Wales (1767–1834), had been trying to interest leading authorities in England in the excellent wool-bearing qualities of the Merino, which he had introduced into Australia in 1797. His eldest son, Edward (later Lt.-Gen. Sir E. MacArthur, K.C.B., and sometime Gov. of Victoria), was serving in the 39th Foot in the Peninsula 1813–14.

7. It is tantalizing to wonder whether Lord Charles won his bet. Napoleon abdicated at the end of the first week in April, but armistice in the south was not concluded until 17 April, by which time the Battle of Toulouse had been fought.

8. Larpent, *Private Journal*, vol. ii, p. 295.

9. Wellington had been hit by a spent ball on the thigh. As he was stretched on the ground for a few minutes to recover, the by-standers, ignorant at first of the slight nature of his wound, broke out unanimously with the despairing remark: 'God God! Who is to get the army out of the country!'
[Combermere, *Memoirs and Correspondence*, vol. i, p. 308.]

10. The Bayonne garrison totalled 14,000; 8,000 with an additional division of 6,000.

11. 500 sail in Passages in April 1814 may sound a high figure but it was realistic. The extremely sheltered, long, narrow, fjord-like inlet close to San Sebastian was the finest harbour on the northern coast of Spain and inevitably became a main supply port. Moreover many additional craft were still in the offing for the bridge of boats at Bayonne.

12. It was one of the sad episodes of the war that the Governor of Bayonne, flouting the ceasefire, launched a powerful yet aimless sortie on 13 April, needlessly causing some 1,750 casualties on both sides (including Sir John Hope wounded and taken prisoner). Bayonne finally surrendered on 26 April.

13. An earlier eye-witness wrote soon after the storm of San Sebastian:
'. . . With the exception of ten or twelve fortunate biuldings, there is nothing left . . . but the blackened walls of its houses and these are falling every instant. . . . How the fire started is uncertain. . . . In a town so constructed as this, there was little chance of its being got under control when kindled.'
[Gomm, *Letters and Journals*, p. 319.]

EPILOGUE

1. *Dorset County Chronicle*, 18 April 1863.

Index

Page numbers in italics refer to references in Biographical Notes and Notes and References

Printed at
Aberdeen University Press

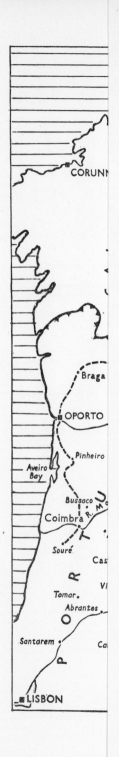